MAGGIE COLVIN'S
Fabulous Fakes

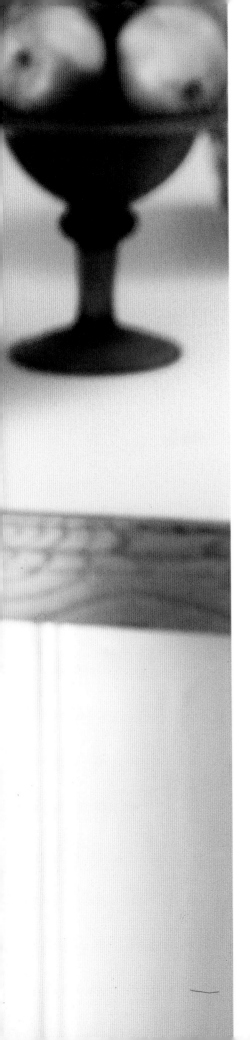

MAGGIE COLVIN'S

Fabulous Fakes

David & Charles

A DAVID & CHARLES BOOK

First published in the UK in 1999
First published in paperback 2002

Distributed in North America
by F&W Publications, Inc.
4700 E. Galbraith Rd.
Cincinnati, OH 45236
1-800-289-0963

A catalogue record for this book is available
from the British Library.

ISBN 0 7153 1316 9 (paperback)

Photography: Lizzie Orme
Step Photography: Sussie Bell
Stylist: Maggie Colvin
Editor: Beverley Jollands
Designer: Bet Ayer

Printed in Italy by Milanostampa SpA
for David & Charles
Brunel House, Newton Abbot, Devon

Contents

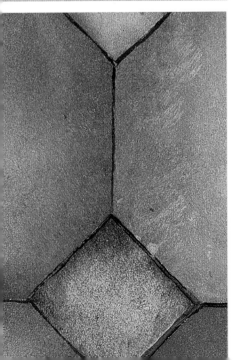

Introduction

Painted illusions can be extraordinarily effective, decorative and fun to execute. They also have an illustrious historical precedent. From Versailles to Blenheim Palace there is hardly a grand house in Europe without a painted sky, a *faux* marble hall, or a classical landscape scene. Let's not pretend it will always last as long or feel the same, but if the real thing is too expensive the exciting likelihood is that you can fake it with paint.

Far from dismissing such effects as poor counterfeits, you can argue that there are even some cases when the fake has an advantage over the real thing. A pretty collection of stencilled china will never get broken. A *faux* stone or mosaic floor can enhance an upstairs room without imposing extra weight on an old structure. Fake tongue and groove boarding can be installed without moving the bathroom fittings. Unlike a real view of the countryside,

a Tuscan landscape painted on cupboard doors can be transported when you move house. Admittedly, murals depicting a Caribbean seascape or a Greek island can never truly replace a view of the real thing, but they are colourful and decorative and, by visual association, they appeal to the escapist in all of us. At best, they trigger off memories of happy holidays that lift your spirits on a dull day.

Another big bonus in favour of faking is the saving to be enjoyed on builders' bills. Most fake effects involve less work than installing the genuine article. This is particularly true of painted wooden panelling, tiles, inlaid stone, marble and mosaics, where your only investment is in time and the cost of a few basic materials like paints, brushes, masking tape and a stencil or two.

When the painted sky really looks like part of a summer's day, or the marble has been mistaken for the real thing, the sense of achievement and artistic satisfaction is immeasurable. If you have never painted a fake the therapeutic spin-off is really impossible to describe. Painting whole rooms takes up lots of energy and is rather like a workout in the gym, with the added advantage that besides losing weight and gaining fitness you obtain tangible rewards for your endeavours.

There are lots of short cuts to make the faking job less arduous. For instance, most fakes will look more convincing if you can incorporate some real elements in the project, such as a real dado rail, proper mouldings, a shelf, or louvred shutters to frame a pretend window, so don't bother to fake these.

Once you have mastered a few simple paint effects, you can extend your skills to mural painting. Painting murals to animate dull spaces or expand space is a well-known decorator's trick, but is nearly always confined to professionals. However, if you use stencils, professional-looking results are guaranteed, even if you doubt your own drawing skills.

Most of the projects in this book require minimal painting skills and very few expensive materials, apart from a softening brush which is invaluable for many paint effects. Most of them were carried out in water-based paints, for the sake of health and convenience, and many include easy short cuts and tips which expert friends have been kind enough to pass on to me.

Basic Techniques

Tips for Planning and Painting

While most paint effects are easy to master following the simple steps shown on the next few pages, mural painting presents more of a challenge. So here are some general guidelines which should help to galvanize and inspire you.

1 The most successful murals are those which appear to extend the room's living space beyond the wall and which make this illusion seem architecturally plausible: elements such as terraces, patios, balconies, flights of garden steps or the continuation of roof beams as if in a conservatory can all be helpful. The perspective of lines of tiles painted on the floor of a pretend patio, for instance, will lead the eye into the mural and, because they are in the foreground, will look like an extension of the real world (see the Tuscan landscape on page 102). If you can match the style of the real floor in the room with the painted floor, so much the better.

2 If you are embarking on your first mural, a board or screen presents a less daunting 'canvas' than a whole wall. It also gives you the option to decide where in the house to place your masterpiece, once it is completed.

3 Finding the right blank wall to paint is unlikely to be difficult: it usually stares you in the face. Garden walls and patio areas are traditionally popular. A conservatory often has a dominating high wall to which the structure has been added. Long passages and windowless rooms such as bathrooms and toilets are obvious contenders for pretend windows. Recessed alcoves on either side of the mantelpiece in a living room can be turned into interesting focal points. Built-in cupboard doors in bedrooms and on landings are favourite locations. Sky ceilings or beach scenes usually go down well in children's bedrooms. Because of the humidity it's inadvisable to hang pictures in bathrooms, so they are strong candidates for murals, particularly seascapes or plant-filled conservatories.

4 It requires thought to integrate and make sense of existing structural elements such as sloping ceilings, doors and windows. If the window has a distinctive characteristic such as an arch, you can echo the shape in other painted features. The Orchard mural on page 112 is a good example. On walls where a solitary window or door is positioned off-centre or to one side, you have the opportunity to improve the architectural proportions. If you double the shape you will end up with a pair of windows, one painted and the other real. A pair of anything creates a desirable symmetry.

The painted window should have a vista to match the real view as far as possible. The same principle could apply in the case of a door. Most doors and windows will not 'float' comfortably in a landscape so you need to create walls around them – even a half-crumbling stone wall can look decorative and atmospheric.

5 You can begin with only the haziest idea of what you would like to achieve, even with an initial doodle on the back of an envelope. You may be inspired by a travel poster or a magazine cutting, or a landscape view found in some classical architectural reference book. At the next stage, you should begin to structure the design to include a foreground, middle · ground and background. It is always a good idea to frame a mural in some way. A framework of trellis and climbing plants placed at the top and a low wall with a row of pots, or a line of grass, at the bottom will make the rest of the scene recede, creating the important illusion of depth.

6 A useful device which will save you time and energy, and also improve the authenticity of any mural, is to incorporate some real architectural features in the illusion. Dado rails, mouldings, skirting boards, window frames, window shelves, shutters and even hinged windows, preferably without glass for safety, can all be included where possible and appropriate.

7 As a general rule, begin by painting the wall in off-white vinyl silk emulsion, which is not too absorbent a base for paint effects. On a piece of graph paper, firm up your design and draw it to scale, so that it can be translated easily on to

the wall. Then, to scale up the outline design on the wall, simply divide the surface into large squares using a soft pencil and straight edge, then copy the outline shapes, drawing them into the appropriate squares.

8 It is usually best to paint the sky first, starting with a band of mid-blue at the top of the mural. Thin the paint with water or glaze as you move towards the horizon, as this part of the sky needs to be palest (see the Tuscan landscape on page 102). As a general rule, use pale colours in the distance, and increase colour intensity as you move towards the foreground. The brightest and darkest colours need to be kept for images nearest to the viewer. When applying colour to seas, lakes or distant hills, always use a soft paint effect like stippling or mutton clothing. The nearest hills need a rougher, more distinct texture, which you can achieve with sponging or ragging.

9 For botch-proof professional success, use stencils to create the important images in the mural. Before painting them, stencil the shapes in several coats of white to obliterate the background colours.

10 For indoor scenes, once the stencils have been coloured in, paint a shadow to one side using an artist's brush and cold tea (or thinned brown paint). Decide on the direction of the light source first. This should reflect the real light source and, to establish its direction, simply place a hand flat against the wall and then move it away a fraction. Note the position of the shadow created by your hand. For outdoor scenes, you can highlight one side of the stencilled shapes with white paint to imitate sunlight.

Sponging

Probably one of the quickest, easiest paint techniques, sponging produces a fresh-looking spattered effect which works on most surfaces, even rough textures such as woodchip wallpaper or concrete. A natural sea sponge will create a more interesting, irregular texture than can be achieved with a synthetic one. There are two basic techniques: sponging on, which is simply sponging the glaze directly onto a painted surface; and sponging off, for which you apply a glaze over a base coat using a brush, then lift it off with the sponge.

Sponging on in layers

Sponging on gives a crisp, airy result, and sponging in layers – using more than one colour – makes for a rich effect which is worth the extra effort. You can either use solid colours (for *trompe l'oeil* effects, layers of different colours make excellent grass or brick textures) or dilute the paint with a glaze, to produce translucent layers, as shown here, for a feeling of depth.

1 Pour two or three different coloured glazes into separate saucers. For the most successful results, choose colours close to each other in the spectrum – mint green, sea green and mauve are shown here. Wet the sponge and wring it out thoroughly to leave it just damp.

2 Starting with the palest colour, dab the sponge over the wall without twisting it while it is in contact with the wall. Change the angle of your wrist as you work to avoid repeat patterns. Apply the first colour lightly to leave space for the other colours and for the base colour to show through.

3 Rinse the sponge thoroughly before applying the second glaze. You can do this without waiting for the first coat to dry, unless you want the option of wiping off mistakes (in this case, apply a coat of clear acrylic varnish after the first coat). Use the darkest colour and work with the same action as before, filling in any gaps and dispersing the spots as evenly as possible. Apply the second glaze lightly, as before, remembering that your final colour will be dominant.

4 The third and final colour should be a mid-tone and will be the overall dominant colour. Apply as before. If you are decorating a whole room, it's best to work in sections. Use a small artist's or stencil brush to get right into the corners of the room.

Sponging off
This technique creates a denser effect than sponging on, and you may find it easier to achieve an even-textured result.

1 Using a large brush, apply the coloured glaze evenly and generously over your base coat.

2 Using a damp sponge, dab over the glaze evenly to remove the brush marks and lift off some of the colour to reveal the base coat. Vary the angle of your wrist as before. Clean the sponge frequently in a bucket of clear water. To sponge off the glaze in the corners of the room, break off a small piece of sponge or use a stencil brush.

Dragging and Flogging

Both these techniques were developed for, and are still used in, wood-graining. A dragging brush which has long bristles is drawn through the glaze in straight vertical lines to produce an extremely elegant striped effect. It is a skilled job to create slick vertical stripes down the full height of a room, so you may prefer to limit the effect to below dado height. Flogging creates a more textured, subtle effect and is used to create the illusion of wood panelling.

1 Mask off the dado rail and skirting board, then apply a thin layer of glaze evenly with a flat brush, starting from the top and working down to the bottom.

2 To cover the area properly from the very top, hold the dragging brush against the wall and press down with the edge of your hand so the tips of the bristles make immediate contact. Draw the brush through the glaze, working from top to bottom and keeping it as flat as possible on the wall. Align the brush by eye with a straight edge such as a door, rather than look-ing at where it is going.

3 For flogging, follow steps 1 and 2, but once the brush has reached the bottom of the wall, work it back on itself, covering the same ground but this time hitting the surface with short sharp strokes, moving upwards as you do so. This will create hairline distortions in the lines of dragging, giving the irregular appearance of wood-grain.

Stippling

This technique yields sophisticated, classic results and, like sponging, it is simple to master. Having applied the glaze, hit the surface with the stippling brush to produce a very fine, even texture of tiny spots, giving a smooth, translucent finish. To show up properly, the glaze needs to have a high concentration of colour, as it should be spread fairly thinly. Stippling looks best on really smooth surfaces because, unlike sponging or colourwashing, every imperfection is likely to show through. For rich effects, like a tropical sea, use a deeply coloured glaze over a base colour just a couple of tones paler. The result will be dense and soft. Wipe the stippling brush with a rag as it becomes overloaded with glaze, and use a fine stencil brush to get into the corners. You should end up with a fine speckled texture. Any specks of dust or air bubbles can be removed while the glaze is wet. Stipple again immediately to restore the even texture.

1 Cover the base coat with a thin layer of glaze, brushing evenly in all directions.

2 Go over the surface once more and, using the tip of the brush, gently push and disperse any heavy brush strokes and lumps of colour.

3 Gripping the stippling brush firmly, hit the surface at a 90° angle with sharp, regular stabbing strokes. Do not move the brush across the glaze, as this will smudge it. Work in small sections: each time you move to a new area, stipple over the edge of the previous area and make sure the effect looks consistent.

Cloth Imprints

Neither ragging nor mutton clothing requires any specialist equipment, and the techniques are similar: a glaze is applied and then manipulated with a dabbing movement.

Ragging

Ragging is usually done with a bunched cotton cloth, but bunched newspaper or even plastic bags can be used. It produces a lively, irregular texture.

 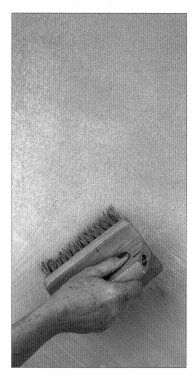 

1 Apply a glaze liberally and evenly over the base coat and draw your brush over the surface in a basket-weave or criss-cross pattern. This will achieve an even-textured coverage ready for ragging.

2 For a really well defined effect, you can, if you choose, stipple the glaze at this point.

3 Bunch up a cotton rag and dab it onto the glaze. Do not rub or smudge it. Lift it off cleanly, leaving the imprint of the rag. After about a dozen dabs, re-form the cloth so it does not become saturated with the glaze. When the rag is completely wet, replace it with a new one. To rag a complete room, you can expect to use up several old sheets. If you are ragging a large area in sections, leave an unworked area to which you can add the next section of glaze.

Mutton clothing

This technique is similar to stippling, but is not such hard work, simply because mutton cloth (which is sold on a roll) is easier to hold than a large stippling brush. Mutton cloth frays easily, so you need to avoid the danger of fibres becoming lodged in the glaze. (If this does happen, lift them off while the glaze is still wet and dab over your fingermarks.) Mutton clothing makes for a softer effect than ragging and is particularly good for shading when painting a mural – when you want a hill to appear to fade into the distance, for instance. It is also a good technique for softening the lines between sky and clouds. For billowy white cloud shapes, use a clean piece of mutton cloth to wipe away the blue glaze completely.

  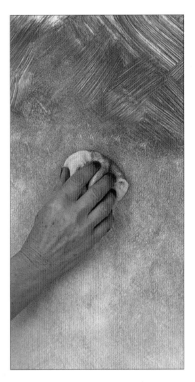

1 Brush the glaze over the base coat as evenly as possible and in a really fine layer.

2 If you are using this technique in a mural, you may wish to shade the colour from dark to light. Apply the glaze more heavily, but still evenly, in the darker areas.

3 Cut a strip of mutton cloth about 30cm/12in long and bunch it, tucking in all the raw edges as you do so. Make sure the surface of the bunched cloth is completely flat. Dab the cloth over the glaze in short clean stabs to produce a cloudy, softly textured effect.

Colourwashing

This technique is quick to apply and, depending on the colours you use, enormously versatile. In stone, grey and mauve it can create a casual, contemporary look, while in terracotta and earth tones it will give a room a rural farmhouse feel. A dark green colourwash makes a good backdrop for antique mahogany furniture, and deep reds give a Chinese look to a room. Depending on your choice of colour you can either deepen or lighten the effect by double colourwashing, and the greater the contrast between the colours the more distinct the distance or three-dimensional effect. You can also colourwash two different colours side by side – this would be appropriate if you were painting an evening sky, for example, where you might juxtapose yellow, pink, orange and dark blue glazes.

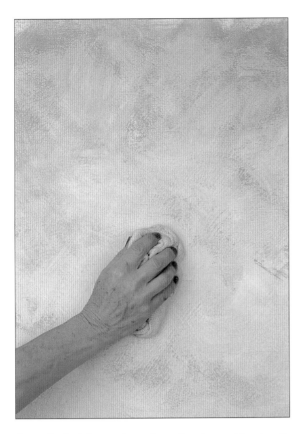

1 Apply the glaze using a large brush, working in all directions over the area. Work on one section at a time, otherwise the glaze may dry out too much before you have time to finish the treatment. When the glaze is slightly tacky, wipe over the wall with a soft cloth scrunched up into a pad with a smooth surface. Wipe in all directions, exposing the base coat without removing the glaze altogether, until all brush marks are obliterated. As the surface of the cloth becomes saturated, re-form the pad and eventually replace the cloth altogether.

2 For double colourwashing, leave the first coat to dry, then apply a second colour in the same way.

3 Keep working until the glaze looks soft and evenly distributed. For an extra cloudy finish, use a softening brush. Hold the brush at 90° to the surface, and flick over the surface with the action of a pendulum, rather as if you were flicking face powder over the skin.

Cutting and Using Stencils

For the bigger mural projects in this book, stencils are used to create the images which would normally demand a high level of artistic skill. Once you have cut the stencils, you can re-use them in several of the projects in the book, and develop your own designs, tailor-made to suit the shape and size of your own rooms. For those without the time or inclination to cut their own stencils, mail order sources of ready-cut designs are listed on page 143.

Cutting ready-designed stencils
To use the stencils printed at the back of this book, take them to a photocopier for enlarging. The size you need will depend on the scale of your project, so first work out the size you want. You can use acetate sheet or stencil card, and both can be cut with a craft knife. Acetate usually lasts longer and is easy to clean and position, but card has the advantage that it is slightly absorbent: if you happen to apply too much paint the edges are less likely to smudge.

If you are using acetate you can also use a heat pen, which is excellent for cutting curves. A craft knife is better for sharp corners and for straight lines. Remember that a heat pen is potentially dangerous. When it is not in use, rest it on a ceramic plate so that the tip is not in contact with any surface.

Whichever method you choose you must be careful not to cut through the bridges of the stencil.

1 To trace the stencil, tape a piece of tracing paper or waxed transparent paper over the design and trace with a fine felt-tipped pen or a soft pencil. A double-layer stencil needs to be cut out of two separate sheets of acetate and it helps to superimpose the second layer on the first to make sure the shapes line up perfectly.

2 To cut acetate with a heat pen, lay the tracing under a piece of glass about 60 x 75cm/24 x 30in and place a sheet of acetate, lightly coated with spray adhesive, on top of the glass. Mask around the edges to make sure it cannot move. Plug in the heat pen and wait a few seconds for it to warm up. Place the point of the pen on a line of the design and move it slowly across the acetate. Trace out the design, moving the heat pen steadily along the line. If you let it rest in one place for too long, it may make an unwanted hole. Once the design is complete, you will find that some shapes fall out and others need to be eased out with your fingers, or even snipped in places with a tiny pair of sharp scissors.

3 To cut a stencil out of acetate with a craft knife, you need to trace the design onto the acetate with a felt-tipped pen.

4 A craft knife is particularly suited to cutting straight edges for designs such as tile stencils. Use a steel rule, held down firmly, and run the craft knife against it to ensure a perfect line.

Stencilling with oil crayons

Oil crayons or sticks create a soft effect like airbrushing. The colours are particularly easy to shade. Unlike paint, they will not run under the edges of the stencil to cause smudging. You need a separate stencil brush for each colour.

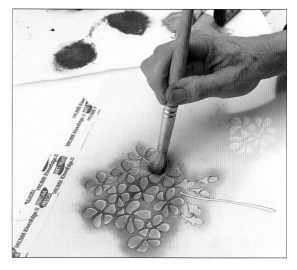

1 Secure the stencil to the surface using either masking tape or a low tack spray which allows for repositioning. Use your stencil as a palette or use a separate piece of paper or card. Rub the crayon onto the paper to break the oil seal, then rub the brush into the crayon to pick up the pigment. Apply it to the stencil using a rotary action. Keep the brush at 90° to the surface at all times.

2 You can build up the colours in layers, and overlap them, turning, say, red and yellow into orange where they meet. For deeper tones, simply apply a second coat. To shade, deepen the colour around the edges of the shape and leave some uncoloured highlights in the centre.

3 If you want an area of clearly defined colour, for instance a clear green for this stem, mask the adjoining areas before applying the colour.

4 Once you have removed the stencil, leave the oil crayon to dry for at least 48 hours before varnishing, otherwise the colour will run. You can also add a three-dimensional effect to a stencilled design by painting a thin tea-coloured line around the outline shape (see the China Shelf on page 80).

Stencilling with paint

Stencil paints allow you more opportunity to vary textures and colour as they can be applied over the stencil with sponges or small rollers as well as brushes. If you are tackling a huge project, small rollers will cover the area quickly.

1 Once you have secured the stencil, take up a small amount of paint on the brush and dab off the excess on a piece of paper towel until it leaves only a misty impression. Dab the brush over the holes of the stencil for a textured effect, or use a rotary action for a smoother finish. Apply lighter colours before shading in darker tones and apply the colour consistently. On these leaves, for instance, pale green is placed along the left-hand side of each leaf, so the sun appears to light them from one direction only.

2 To shade, dab the brush in a second, brighter colour. Here, a darker green is applied along the right-hand side of the leaves to balance the highlights on the other side and create a three-dimensional effect. If the colours appear too brash, you can go over the work once it is dry with a thin wash of gold or light brown. Alternatively, varnish the finished work, leave to dry, then go over the entire work with a white or off-white glaze.

3 To create a painted look, you can paint out the bridges in the stencil in an appropriate colour and add further details with a fine brush. Here, the veins are being painted in a pale green. You can also use a fine brush to add extra details and highlights after removing the stencil to bring the design to life like real sunlight. Add darker tones of the main colour to exaggerate the shady side of the object.

Wonderful Walls

Tongue and Groove Boarding

Painted directly onto plaster walls, limewashed tongue and groove boarding is a good way to decorate a kitchen without much effort, and at a fraction of the cost of real timber. Using a white glaze over a pale grey background yields amazingly sophisticated results, quite minimalist and chic, yet not too stark. Add a real dado rail before you begin painting to make the deception more convincing. If the walls are slightly uneven (though not too much so)

they will add extra interest and texture to the finished result. It is possible to adapt this effect to reproduce colourwashed timber, simply by altering the background colour (see the Secret Door Alcove on page 84).

vinyl silk emulsion in mid-grey
medium paintbrush
clear acrylic varnish
15cm/6in wide plank to fit between dado and
      skirting board
carpenter's pencil ·
1cm/½in masking tape
white emulsion paint
acrylic scumble glaze
wood-grainer
comb with serrated edge

1 Apply two coats of grey paint, leaving them to dry between coats. Apply a coat of clear acrylic varnish to give you a non-absorbent base which improves the definition of the wood-grain. Using a plank as a guide to width, rule vertical lines with the carpenter's pencil over the area of wall to be decorated. Apply a vertical strip of masking tape over each pencil line.

2 Mix white emulsion paint and acrylic scumble glaze in equal parts. Working on one board at a time, apply the white glaze between the lines of masking tape, drawing the brush from top to bottom, parallel with the masking tape.

3 Starting at the top and next to the edge of the masking tape, draw the wood-grainer through the glaze in one continuous motion, rocking it very slightly as you draw. This produces the wood-grain texture. Wipe the build-up of glaze off the grainer.

4 Draw the serrated comb from top to bottom along the outside edge of the wood-grain, and change the angle as you go, to produce extra woody, wobbly textures to enhance the illusion.

5 When the glaze is dry, remove the masking tape to reveal stripes of plain grey.

6 Load an artist's brush with white emulsion paint and draw it down the middle of each narrow grey stripe to create a straight highlight. Use the edge of the plank as a straight edge. This will create the illusion of the narrow ridge which joins tongue and groove boarding. As an option you can also brush on extra parallel lines of dark grey on either side of the white. Leave the paint to dry, then protect your work with two coats of acrylic varnish.

Stonewalling

Stonewalling, like sky ceilings, has
a highly respectable classical pedigree
as a decorative technique and still
commands a universal following. It is
undeniably distinguished and grand,
and when cleverly used, can improve
unsatisfactory proportions.

Contrary to what you would expect,
its three-dimensional character seems to
expand the feeling of space rather than
diminish it, so it is well suited to many
halls and dining rooms and makes an ideal base for a mural. Its timeless style
seems to fit comfortably with antique and modern furniture alike.

There are many different recipes for this effect, but here is one of the
simplest and most successful, using hand-cut masking tape which gives a
slightly uneven and more realistic look to the joints in the stonework.

Although this effect can be executed in acrylics, an oil glaze tinted with
yellow ochre and raw umber yields better visual results and of course is more
hard-wearing so will withstand the traffic in a hallway.

measuring tape
pencil
extra long steel rule or length of wooden moulding
cardboard
scissors
plywood offcut
5cm/2in masking tape
craft knife
oil or acrylic scumble glaze, plain or in buff colour
artist's oil colours in yellow ochre, raw umber and
    black
paint kettle
10–15cm/4–6in wide brush
old newspapers
block brush
softening brush
varnish (optional)
cloths

2 On a plywood offcut, stick several rows of 5cm/2in masking tape side by side and use a craft knife and a steel rule or length of wooden moulding to cut it into thin ribbons about 3mm/⅛in wide. Remove the tape from the board and stick to the wall over all the pencilled lines.

1 Divide the height of the wall to be painted into three, four or five equal block heights, depending on the size of the room. Large blocks look grandest. Mark all horizontal lines first, using a pencil and straight edge. Cut a piece of cardboard to fit between the horizontal lines and cut it into a rectangle to determine the size of each individual stone – any proportion will do, as many different ones are used in stonework. Rule a line through the middle of the card to use as a guide. Place the card between the horizontal lines and use as a ruler to mark off the vertical lines. Note that the middle pencil lines should align with the edges of the blocks above and below, following the pattern of real stonework. Draw over the dado rail if applicable.

3 Mix a buff-coloured glaze, using yellow ochre and raw umber, and apply with a wide brush to one stone at a time. Mix a little black into some of the glaze to produce a darker colour on the side of your paint kettle, and occasionally pick this up in the brush and apply it to the stonework to produce variety of tone.

4 To create a random, stone-like texture, take a sheet of newspaper, place it flat onto a stone and brush over with a block brush. Lift off the newspaper immediately and soften any areas which look too much like solid colour. Work on one stone at a time, and not adjacent ones, as this will help to produce variety.

5 Half-cover some stones with newspaper, and do not cover others at all – simply stipple them with a block brush. This will ensure the kind of randomness which exists in real masonry. Use the same technique to paint the skirting board. When dry, lift off the masking tape. If you used an acrylic glaze, varnish to protect it. As an optional extra you can rule a dark line along the bottom and to one side of each block, depending on the angle of your light source. Colour the dado rail to match, by applying the same glaze and wiping off gently with a cloth.

Velvet and Linen Effect

Glamorous fabric-lined walls are the stuff of Hollywood dreams and look luxuriously unattainable to anyone on an average budget, so a simple copy in paint is worth mastering. This method of producing a crushed velvet effect in stripes is incredibly simple and cheap to produce, mainly using masking tape and old newspaper. The technique used below the dado rail, a chic linen check, is even simpler, so if you do not want the impact of stripes, it is a good option for a cool, uncluttered look.

Varying the colour combinations will dramatically alter the end results: for a plusher, historical feel, you could try a range of dusty pinks and crimsons

on a beige base coat. Or for a more contemporary style, use a range of creams and pale yellows on an off-white base coat. To authenticate the fake, the fabric upholstery braid which takes the place of conventional picture and dado rails is absolutely vital, as real fabric stretched onto the wall is always edged with braid. For an even more opulent finish, you could use fringing or a tassel braid.

MATERIALS AND EQUIPMENT

off-white vinyl silk emulsion paint
large paintbrush
pencil
straight edge
2.5cm/1in and 5cm/2in wide masking tape
plumb line
15cm/6in wide plank about 1.2m/4ft long with
    U-shaped handle attached to the middle
5cm/2in wide moulding about 1.2m/4ft long
acrylic scumble glaze in turquoise, orange and
    yellow
15cm/6in wide paintbrush
old newspapers
block brush
bin bag
hairdryer (if needed)
polyurethane varnish (optional)
old 5cm/2in wide brush
scissors

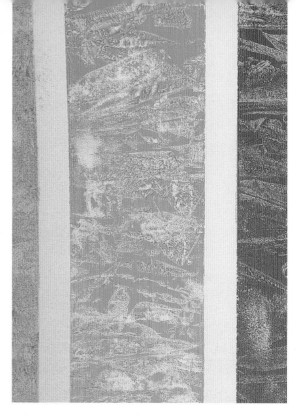

1 Paint the walls in off-white vinyl silk emulsion and draw a horizontal line around the room at dado height. Mask the line with 2.5cm/1in tape. Use the 15cm/6in plank as a guide to rule the wide stripes and the 5cm/2in wide piece of moulding to rule the narrow stripes. Use a plumb line to draw a vertical line down the wall, then rule alternating vertical stripes above dado height all round the room. Mask over the narrower stripe with the masking tape.

2 Paint the wide stripes in three different glaze colours using a 15cm/6in brush and working from top to bottom. You may be able to treat two or three stripes at once, depending on how quickly you work.

3 While the glaze is still wet, fold a sheet of newspaper to create rough concertina folds just like a fan, and place this horizontally across the stripes. Flatten the paper against the glaze using a block brush.

4 Lift off the newspaper immediately, leaving an imprint which looks like crushed velvet. When the sheet of newspaper becomes saturated in the glaze throw it into the bin bag (to avoid getting paint everywhere) and use a new sheet. Leave to dry, then remove the masking tape. If you have difficulty with this, use a hairdryer to soften the adhesive and lift off the tape gently so as not to remove any paint. If the room will be used by small children, protect the finished effect with a coat of polyurethane varnish.

5 For the linen effect below the dado, half cut away some of the hairs of an old paintbrush to produce a finely jagged edge which will create a comb pattern. Apply the yellow glaze and drag the brush from top to bottom over the whole area.

6 To create the woven look, run the brush horizontally over the wet glaze. This will create a criss-cross weave that looks just like linen. Work in sections so the glaze does not dry before you treat it. Protect the work with varnish.

Sky Ceiling

The notion of painting a ceiling to look like a sky goes back many centuries and has never really been out of fashion. Painted skies are particularly suited to sloping attic rooms, wrapping up the space in a romantic, airy canopy and providing an extra dimension of light and space. This tiny kitchen is a good example. In standard box rooms, it can be a good idea to install a picture rail and treat the area above it to match the sky ceiling.

Of all the many different sky paint effect recipes, this must be one of the simplest and easiest to live with. Just two glaze colours, applied over a white base, are mutton clothed into soft, billowy cloud shapes with a hint of sunshine peeping through. For greater theatrical impact the effect can be beefed up by adding white, to shape more definite clouds, and darker blue for contrast. By adding touches of grey, mauve and orange it can be evolved into a more dramatic sunset sky. Or, with a darker spectrum of blues and tiny star stencils, you can use exactly the same technique to make a dark night sky. Stars can also be faked with fibre-optic lights embedded in the ceiling.

white vinyl silk emulsion paint
large paintbrush
pale blue pre-tinted glaze, or acrylic
    scumble glaze mixed with artist's acrylic
    colours in ultramarine, titanian white and
    Paynes grey
long-handled roller (for high ceilings) or ladder
block brush
mutton cloth
cloths
pale yellow pre-tinted glaze or acrylic scumble
    glaze mixed with yellow ochre and white
softening brush

1 Paint the ceiling and sloping walls with two coats of white vinyl silk emulsion paint. Apply blue glaze in random strokes, leaving white patches in between. Use a roller on a long handle if the ceiling is very high, or a brush if you can reach. Work in 1m/3ft-square sections as most acrylic glazes begin to set in about 3–10 minutes, depending on the temperature of the room. The cooler the glaze, the longer it will remain malleable.

2 While the glaze is still wet, break up and obliterate the brush strokes with the block brush, softening the break between blue and white patches. Rub the mutton cloth into the glaze in a circular motion to make fairly definite cloudy shapes, revealing the white paint below. Go over the whole area again with mutton cloth to give a soft, airy effect.

3 Even after the glaze has dried, you can rub it away with a damp cloth to make more cloud shapes. Alternatively, if you want to beef up the colour, you can add more of the blue glaze, or even a darker shade of blue if you wish.

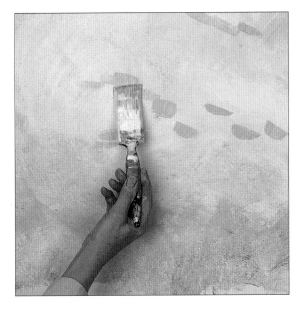

4 Using an ordinary brush loaded with creamy yellow glaze, fill in around the edges of some of the clouds. Use mutton cloth to fudge the edges and blend the clouds into the sky. This step will create the effect of sun shining through the clouds.

5 To soften the effect further, you can go over the yellow glaze with a softening brush if you wish.

Gingham Covered Walls

A bedroom lined with fabric is a luxury few can afford but of course, like most things, it can be faked in paint. This check effect has a fresh, contemporary feel in bright, light colours – though it can change dramatically with a different palette. In traditional dark greens, blues and reds, it will produce a dramatic tartan effect, and in pale off-white tones, a neutral minimalist look. The obvious way to find inspiration is to pick three colours from the fabric used in the room and use the dominant colour for the background glaze. Here, the blue background echoes the bright blue stripe in the flowery chintz, and the stripes pick up accent colours in sharp green and yellow. Instead of conventional wooden mouldings, you could use a fabric braid to edge the effect.

The first stage of this technique is produced without masking tape, and if you prefer an easy soft effect, you can leave it like this. Adding the other colours is a labour of love, but you could cut the workload by drawing much larger checks or confining the effect to below or above a dado.

If you size the checks to the width of a plank of wood with a handle attached, the initial drawing is much quicker. The walls should first be painted in white vinyl silk emulsion. If they are already painted in ordinary emulsion, apply a coat of clear acrylic varnish to provide a suitable surface.

measuring tape

plumb line

2.5cm/1in wide wooden moulding about 1.2m/
    4ft long

pencil

15cm/6in wide plank about 1.2m/4ft long with
    U-shaped handle attached to the middle

acrylic scumble glaze in ultramarine, lime green
    and pale yellow-green

large paintbrush

dragging brush

mutton cloth

2.5cm/1in wide foam paint pad, cut to size if
    necessary

masking tape

stencil brush

acrylic varnish

1 Working on one wall at a time, find the middle of the wall and with a plumb line, wooden moulding and pencil, draw a vertical line from top to bottom. Place the wide plank flat on the wall against this line and rule a second vertical line along the opposite edge from top to bottom. Place the narrow moulding against this line and rule a third line. Continue the vertical lines until you have covered the wall, alternating with wide and narrow widths of timber. Draw the horizontal lines in the same way, starting from the top of the wall and using the narrow moulding first.

2 Working in one small area at a time, say a group of nine checks, apply the background blue glaze all over with an ordinary paintbrush, working in vertical strokes. Drag the glaze to create a fine striped texture. Wrap a piece of mutton cloth around the paint pad and secure it with tape or an elastic band to keep it clear of your work. While the glaze is still wet, draw the pad along the narrow stripes. This will lift some of the glaze, producing a lighter blue woven imprint. Don't worry if the lines look slightly wobbly as this will help imitate the weave of real fabric. You will need to rewrap the mutton cloth over the pad as it becomes saturated in the glaze. Cover the horizontals as well as the verticals. Continue this process in sections until the whole wall is covered in squares.

3 When the wall is completely dry, you can choose to mask a 2.5cm/1in wide vertical stripe next to the pale blue stripe or to work freehand. Either way, load a stencil brush with lime green glaze and draw a second parallel line to one side of each pale blue line. Reload the brush frequently to create a smoothly dragged line. While the glaze is still wet, go over it as before with mutton cloth wrapped around the paint pad. Wobble the lines to make them slightly irregular like a real weave. Repeat the process until all the vertical stripes are completed, then paint the horizontal stripes.

4 Using pale yellow-green, paint the stripes on the opposite side of the initial pale blue stripes. When all the vertical stripes are painted, paint the horizontal stripes in the same way. In areas likely to get knocked about, such as passages and halls, you should protect the finished effect with a coat of varnish. Use matt for a linen effect, or satin for a glazed chintz look.

Pine Panelling

The warmth and luxury of a wood-panelled room is undeniable. Failing the real thing, you can achieve the illusion of opulent panelling with a simple paint recipe involving a minimum of decorating skills. It is guaranteed to give even the most featureless modern room amazing architectural distinction.

Incorporating a real dado rail and skirting board is the key to a convincing deception, and the size and position of the panels is also important. As with all faking, it helps to find real examples to analyse. Avoid panels of a uniform size, which look mass-produced. Instead, copy the stately home format, in which the shape and size of each panel is determined by the room's own proportions and the position of existing doors and windows.

The walls are usually divided horizontally by a dado rail set at about a third of the height of the wall. In the example shown here, the area below the wall has been divided into three panels of the same height, but of different widths, with a wider central panel flanked by a pair of narrower ones. The panels above are organized to occupy the remaining two-thirds of the wall space and reflect the width of the panels below. The room should be painted first in two coats of off-white vinyl silk emulsion.

pencil

paper

measuring tape

straight edge

template for plank width
     (such as a standard-size envelope)

white spirit

cloths

masking tape

acrylic scumble glaze tinted with a mixture of
     yellow ochre and raw umber artist's acrylic
     colours

medium paintbrush

15cm/6in wide brush

wood-grainer with comb attachment

dragging brush

emulsion or acrylic paint in black and white

angular fitch brush or small, flat artist's brush

moulding for dado rail

saw

drill

wall plugs

screws

screwdriver

wood filler

sandpaper

clear acrylic varnish

1 For each wall, make a rough diagram to determine the size and position of the panels. Mark the middle of the wall with a light pencil line. Using a pencil and straight edge, mark the position and depth of the dado rail by ruling two horizontal lines to encircle the room. Mark out one large centre panel with two flanking panels, using the template to determine the gaps between them, the skirting board and dado rail. Rub away any superfluous pencil lines using white spirit on a cloth.

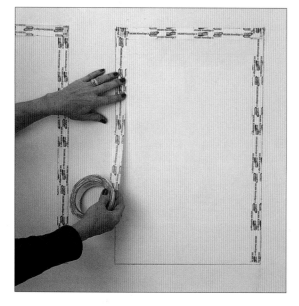

2 Using masking tape, tape around all the pencil lines masking the dado rail and panels, so that the frames are ready for wood-graining.

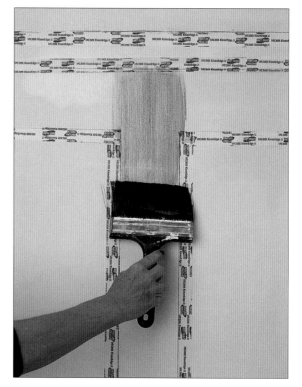

3 Apply the pine-coloured glaze as evenly as possible using an ordinary brush, covering one of the upright timbers only. Using the wide brush, drag the glaze vertically in one direction.

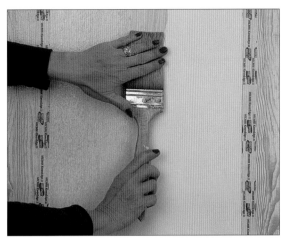

4 Draw the wood-grainer through the wet glaze, working from top to bottom and rocking it very slightly at intervals. Use a cloth to remove the excess glaze as it builds up on the grainer. Run the comb attached to the grainer along the edge of the 'plank', turning it at an angle as you do so. This will add a finely textured undulation typical of the edges of pine boarding. Repeat the process to create the horizontal timbers, running the full width of the wall. At the ends define the edges neatly, creating the impression of two separate pieces of timber butting onto each other.

5 Leave the paint to dry, then remove the masking tape and mask over the frames along their inside edges. Using the wide brush, apply the glaze as before and with the dragging brush create a flogged effect following the instructions on page 12.

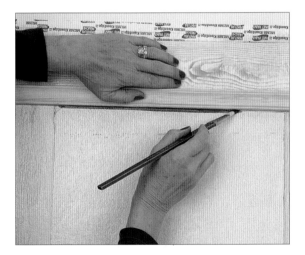

6 Paint highlights and shadows around the panels to bring the illusion dramatically to life. In this room the main light source is to the right, but you should adapt the pattern of light and shade to fit in with the position of your own windows. Add some tinted glaze to the black acrylic paint to soften and dilute it. Then, pressing a straight edge against the wall, run a fully loaded artist's brush along the edge, painting a line 5mm/¼in thick around the inside top and right-hand edges of the panel. Leave to dry.

7 Place masking tape at a 45° angle over the ends of both black lines to create neatly mitred corners where the highlights and shadows meet. Paint the highlights using white acrylic mixed with the tinted glaze. Treat the outer edges in the same way but highlight the top and right-hand side, and shade the left and bottom edges of the panels. Cut and fit the dado rail. Decorate it to match the panels by wiping the glaze along the rail with an ordinary paintbrush. When dry, varnish your finished work to protect it.

Fabulous Floors

Swedish Wood Floor

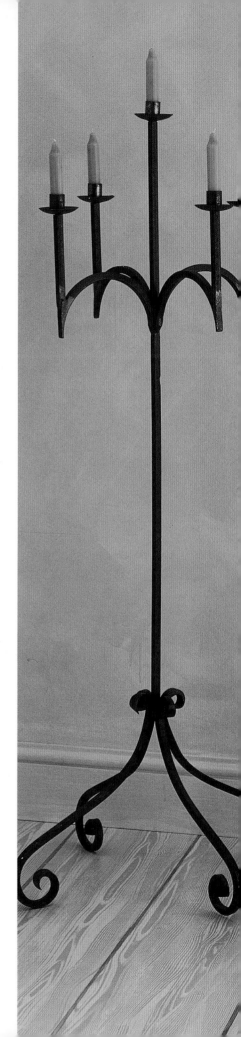

The pale, neutral style associated with Swedish good looks is easy to live with and in much demand. A natural wood floor is an essential part of that idiom, along with off-white distressed furniture, soft, pale voile curtains and white sofas. As wide floorboards are an exclusive asset found only in period houses, this illusion is worth attempting and would upgrade the architectural quality of any room, however small.

The technique itself is not difficult, the only challenge is the energy needed to tackle a whole floor with a paintbrush and to keep family and friends off the premises during drying times.

Using oil paints will increase the lifespan of this effect, though acrylics are faster drying and low-odour. The most important part of the job is varnishing the finished work with a top quality floor varnish. As an extra foil, washable cotton rugs to protect the busiest parts of the room are a good idea and fit in well with the style.

You may need to cover the existing floor with plywood, and a lining of felt may be necessary over concrete – best consult your builder.

pine-coloured paint, either oil-based eggshell or
   vinyl silk emulsion
15cm/6in paintbrush
string
drawing pins
20cm/8in wide floorboard to use as template
pencil
measuring tape
5mm/¼in signwriter's tape
craft knife
steel rule
white oil or acrylic scumble glaze
extra wide wood-grainer with comb attachment
cloths
softening brush (optional)
hairdryer (if needed)
brown oil or emulsion paint
length of wooden moulding
brush with angular tip designed for dry-brushing
floor varnish

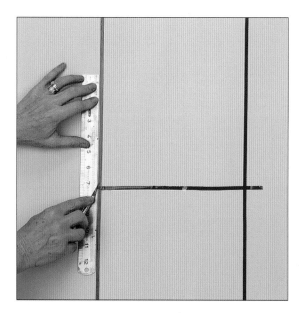

1 Paint the prepared floor with two coats of sandy
pine colour. Find the middle of the room by pinning
two lengths of string diagonally across it. Beginning
from the middle and working outwards, use the
floorboard template to rule straight parallel lines.
Decide on a length for the boards – say about
2m/6ft – and rule a line widthways to denote the
end of one board and the beginning of the next.
These joins should be staggered at random. Stick
signwriter's tape over the ruled lines. To cut the ends
neatly, use a craft knife and steel rule.

2 Unless you are using oil glaze, which has a far
longer working time, tackle one floorboard at a time.
Using a wide brush, cover it evenly with white glaze
working in the direction of the grain. While the glaze
is still wet, draw the large wood-grainer through it
over the middle of the plank, in one continuous
motion, rocking it gently to create a pine pattern.
Wipe the grainer from time to time to take off the
excess glaze.

3 Draw the comb attachment through any untreated areas of the glaze, twisting it gently to produce patterns that are tighter but still irregular, like wood-grain. Repeat if necessary, working near the edges of the plank. If you wish, you can soften the effect with a softening brush, flicking the brush lightly across the work, but also working up and down the grain so as not to lose the first pattern. Leave this first plank to dry while you start work on a second plank some distance away from the first.

4 Leave the floor to dry thoroughly, then remove the masking tape. If the tape threatens to remove paint as you take it off, direct a hairdryer onto it to melt the adhesive. If necessary you can touch up the effect with a small brush before varnishing. Mix the brown paint with a small amount of white glaze (about 8:1) and, using a piece of moulding as a straight edge, load the artist's brush and go over the dividing lines. The glaze will help the flow. Do not make these lines too dark or heavy. When all the paint is dry, apply the floor varnish.

Mosaic Bathroom Floor

Dazzlingly colourful, this stencilled *faux* mosaic floor dramatically transforms a tiny cottage bathroom. A fraction of the weight and expense of the real thing, it is remarkably effective and easy to paint, using three simple stencils which can be arranged to fit a floor of any size or shape.

The main stencil is a large mosaic pattern in a snail's shell arrangement, based on a Roman design. The border has a corner motif in the form of a jumping fish, and a straight matching fish border sized to the same width, based on the symbol used by the early Christian church. Once you have juggled their positions, any gaps in the border are filled with smaller tiles of plain mosaic tesserae. Mosaic designs need to be cut in a relaxed, irregular way, which is best achieved using acetate and a heat pen.

To create a bright, Mediterranean swimming-pool effect, stencil over a pure white base using oil crayons. These produce dazzling translucent colours and,

when shaded, look remarkably similar to real mosaic. Unlike paint, crayons will not run or smudge under the stencil bridges. You can intensify the colour with a second coat if you like.

photocopier
tracing paper
felt-tipped pen
acetate sheet
glass sheet
spray adhesive
masking tape
heat pen
white vinyl silk emulsion paint
large paintbrush
measuring tape
pencil
straight edge
oil crayons in blue, bright turquoise, yellow
    and red
stencil brushes
string
drawing pins
matt polyurethane varnish

1 Enlarge and cut the stencils at the back of the book following the instructions on pages 18 and 19. The border and corner design have two layers, so you need to cut each separately. In addition, trace and cut out a straight row of four single tesserae to fill in gaps in the border design. Paint the entire floor with two or three coats of white vinyl silk emulsion and leave to dry. Rule an 11cm/4¼in border all around the room, and around the front of the bath, basin, loo and bidet if this seems to work best. Place the first layer of the corner fish design in one corner. Mark the repeat positions for the straight fish border design. Unless they happen to fit perfectly, rejig them so they are equally spaced, and mark any gaps to be filled in with individual mosaic pieces, which can be repeat-stencilled side by side to fill in bigger gaps.

2 Lightly spray the back of the corner fish stencil with adhesive. Lay it in position and colour in the outer edges with the bright blue crayon. Colour the inner pieces of the mosaic turquoise.

3 Position the second layer of the corner stencil and colour with the yellow crayon. Add red along the back of the fish. Where these colours overlap the fish will look orange. Leave the underside of the fish yellow.

4 Stencil the border design in the same way, with blue along the outer edges and turquoise in between. Colour the fish to match the corner piece. Fill in any gaps with the line of four tesserae coloured to match the border – blue along the outside edges and turquoise in the middle.

5 Find the middle of the floor using two pieces of string pinned in the corners of the room and stretched diagonally across it. Make a pencil mark at the centre point where the strings cross. Butt the large tile onto this, and colour with the turquoise crayon. To create the variation typical of real mosaic, shade some areas with blue. Give the centre a second coat to intensify the colour but leave lighter patches to vary the texture. Reposition the large tile and repeat until you reach the outer edges of the room.

6 To fit the tiles into the outer edges you may need to halve, quarter or diminish them in some way, depending on the gaps left to fill. To do this, simply mask off part of the design using masking tape. Around the base of the loo or basin, use masking tape placed diagonally across a single tessera to fill in curved corners. When complete, leave the floor to dry for at least 24 hours before applying three coats of polyurethane floor varnish. This is most important as the crayons are oil-based and will otherwise dissolve into the varnish and run.

Inlaid Stone Floor

An inlaid stone floor combining slate, flagstone and brick is a hugely desirable luxury and although the fake variety will not last as long, the results are stunning and well worth the effort. The design can be painted directly onto floorboards or smooth concrete. Easier still, paint directly onto plywood, which you can cut to the size of flagstones if you wish. In a hall, kitchen or dining room it creates an authentic country style and is easy to clean.

For a more lasting finish, you should use oil-based paints for the job, but you can use acrylic and then apply an oil-based varnish for extra protection. The rule is that you can apply oil-based over water-based paints but not the other way round. If you remember to keep any leftover glaze in a sealed container, you always have the option of touching up the floor at a later date. Choose a colour scheme to suit your kitchen units, and for inspiration look at real examples in your local tile showroom. Shades of pink and rust or terracotta look good with natural wood, while shades of grey, slate and black would suit a more high-tech kitchen.

off-white eggshell or vinyl silk emulsion paint
large paintbrush
pencil
5cm/2in wide length of wooden moulding
1cm/½in masking tape
measuring tape
oil glaze
paint kettles
artist's oil colours: raw umber, yellow ochre,
    Venetian red, ultramarine, Paynes grey, black
    and white
block brush
newspaper or tissue paper
turpentine
cloths
cosmetic foam pad
oil-based varnish

1 Paint the floor with two coats of eggshell or vinyl silk emulsion in creamy white. Decide whether you want the border to butt up to the edge of the floor, or whether to create an inset rectangular border and fill in the outer edges with large solid blocks to match the middle. A lot depends on how many alcoves and awkward shapes there are to negotiate in the room. This design butts directly up to the base of the kitchen units. Position and rule the border to suit, by taping two parallel lines of masking tape about 7.5cm/3in apart all the way round the room. Mark a second parallel line 23cm/9in from the first and mask with tape. Fill in with flagstones of a convenient size to fit the central area. Mask off the corners by sticking down two parallel lines 7.5cm/3in apart at a diagonal. Divide the remaining border into equal lengths. Draw in the zig-zag design with a straight edge and pencil, and stick the masking tape along the pencilled lines.

2 Mix a brick-coloured glaze: to a breakfast cup of glaze add a 5cm/2in squirt each of raw umber and Venetian red from tubes of colour. Apply the glaze to the outer and inner border with an ordinary brush, then stipple it to break up the brush strokes using a block brush. Be careful not to go over the edge of the masking tape. Bunch a sheet of newspaper or tissue paper at the bottom to make a half fan shape and lay this on the wet glaze. Sweep across the back of the paper with the block brush and lift off immediately. The imprint of the scrunched-up paper will leave a mottled pattern like natural brick. Be careful to vary the position of the paper. If some patches seem over-defined, stipple them to soften using the stippling brush.

3 Mix a blue slate colour glaze using the same proportion of glaze to artist's colours but this time using French ultramarine and Paynes grey. Repeat the same technique, applying it to the zig-zag pattern. Be careful to contain the glaze within the masking tape. Any mistakes can be wiped off with turpentine. Leave to dry thoroughly for 24 hours.

4 Mix a sand colour glaze in the same proportions as above but using yellow ochre, raw umber and white oil colours. Apply the glaze to the triangular sections and the large stones. Stipple as before, but take extra care to remove brush strokes with the block brush, as these will show up more on the larger stones than the narrow borders.

5 Use paper to create texture as before, making sure you vary the position of the paper and leave some sections untouched to create the sort of variety found in natural stone. Continue until all the stone-work is mottled. Leave the buff colour to dry.

6 When the floor is dry, remove the masking tape. Finally dip a cosmetic foam pad into some grey paint (mix white and black) and run it along the white lines to look like grouting. Apply three coats of varnish, allowing it to dry between coats.

Special
Features

Iron Bedhead

In a cramped bedroom where you need a double bed but there is simply no room for bedside tables, building a deep shelf behind the bedhead is a great solution. It will house all the necessary clobber – books, lamps, clock – that you need alongside you. To decorate it, a pretend wrought-iron bedstead takes up no extra space and transforms an ordinary divan into a luxurious, eye-catching feature.

Only two stencils are required for this project, a 'balcony' stencil and an S-shape, which can be found at the back of the book. Using oil crayons will give you a tough, long-lasting effect which won't easily be worn away when it is leant against.

Using verdigris colours – green, blue, black and gold – produces a sumptuous mellow effect which shows up well against a soft terracotta wash. As verdigris is produced when copper tarnishes over the years, stencil the bedhead with the gold crayon first, and age it with the other colours. The bedposts can be stencilled or real. These are made from old curtain poles topped with cupboard doorknobs.

MATERIALS AND EQUIPMENT

off-white vinyl silk emulsion paint
10cm/4in wide paintbrush
pre-tinted terracotta glaze
mutton cloth
measuring tape
pencil
straight edge
straight and flexible masking tape
large plate or circular tray
oil crayons in gold, marine blue, sap green
    and black
stencil brushes
photocopier
acetate sheet
heat pen
glass sheet
spray adhesive
dowelling, brackets and knobs (optional)
cup (optional)
acrylic varnish

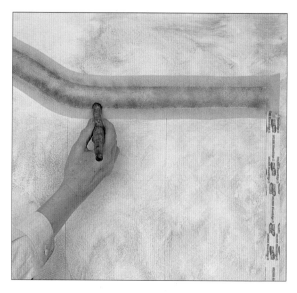

1 Paint the walls with two coats of off-white silk emulsion, then colourwash following the instructions on pages 16 and 17. Measure from the floor to the top of the mattress and mark a horizontal line to correspond with the width and position of the bed. Mark a second horizontal line at the height of the balcony stencil. Mask two vertical lines to enclose a rectangle. Find the centre of the top line and using a large plate or circular tray as a template, draw a semicircular shape for the arched top of the bedhead. On either side of the arch draw two horizontal straight lines to the width of the bed.

2 Draw a second, parallel line around the curved top about 5cm/2in away and mask the outer edges with flexible tape. Colour in the rail using the gold oil crayon. Reinforce the shape by shading the outer edges in blue and black to create a three-dimensional effect. Divide the bedhead into six equal sections to match the width of the balcony stencil and mark with a light pencil line or mask with narrow tape.

3 Enlarge and cut the two stencils at the back of the book to fit the bedhead. Mask off one straight edge on the right-hand side of the balcony stencil. Spray the back of the balcony stencil with adhesive and butt it onto the left-hand side of the bedhead. Fill in with gold, then dab and rub on blue and green alternately, using a separate stencil brush for each colour. Concentrate on joins, where tarnish habitually sets in. Create extra depth and shading with the black crayon around the outside edges to produce highlights in the middle.

4 Position the large S-shaped stencil inside the balcony stencil and colour to match. Reverse the stencil to complete the pattern.

5 Reposition the balcony stencil to decorate the middle of the bedhead with a star. Stencil the tops of the two curves adjoining the star to complete the design. For the bedposts you can either attach wooden dowelling to the wall with brass brackets and screw wooden knobs to the top, or you can stencil the shapes directly to the wall. For the knobs, draw circles using a cup as a template and mask with flexible tape. For the posts, simply draw two vertical lines, mask and then paint to match the rest of the bedhead. Protect the work with acrylic varnish.

Kilim Wall Rug

Palaces in India, castles in Europe and grand houses everywhere in the world boast their fair share of rich tapestry hangings and sumptuous rugs. Their contemporary offspring is the kilim, which like all the best classic designs will mix with any style.

The joy of this creative cheat is its flexibility; you can stencil it onto clean, sanded floorboards or use it to fill an awkward gap over a stairwell instead of conventional pictures which are vulnerable to children pushing their way upstairs. You could also use it to decorate a blank wall behind your bed, or position the design above a bath or sofa. Using fabric paints, you can stencil it onto canvas or silk and make unique curtains or bedhangings and decorate the walls to match.

The design is built up using several rows of different border patterns edged with a tasselled fringe, so you can use as few or as many different patterns as you like. If you don't want the labour of cutting them out, sources for ready-made designs are listed at the back of the book. Although earth brown and terracotta colours are traditional, they can be changed to suit any individual room scheme. Brighter, bolder colours make for a more modern look, or a mixture of black, gold and Chinese red would look oriental. For a hint of extra three-dimensional authenticity, a real brass hook and tassels are important accessories.

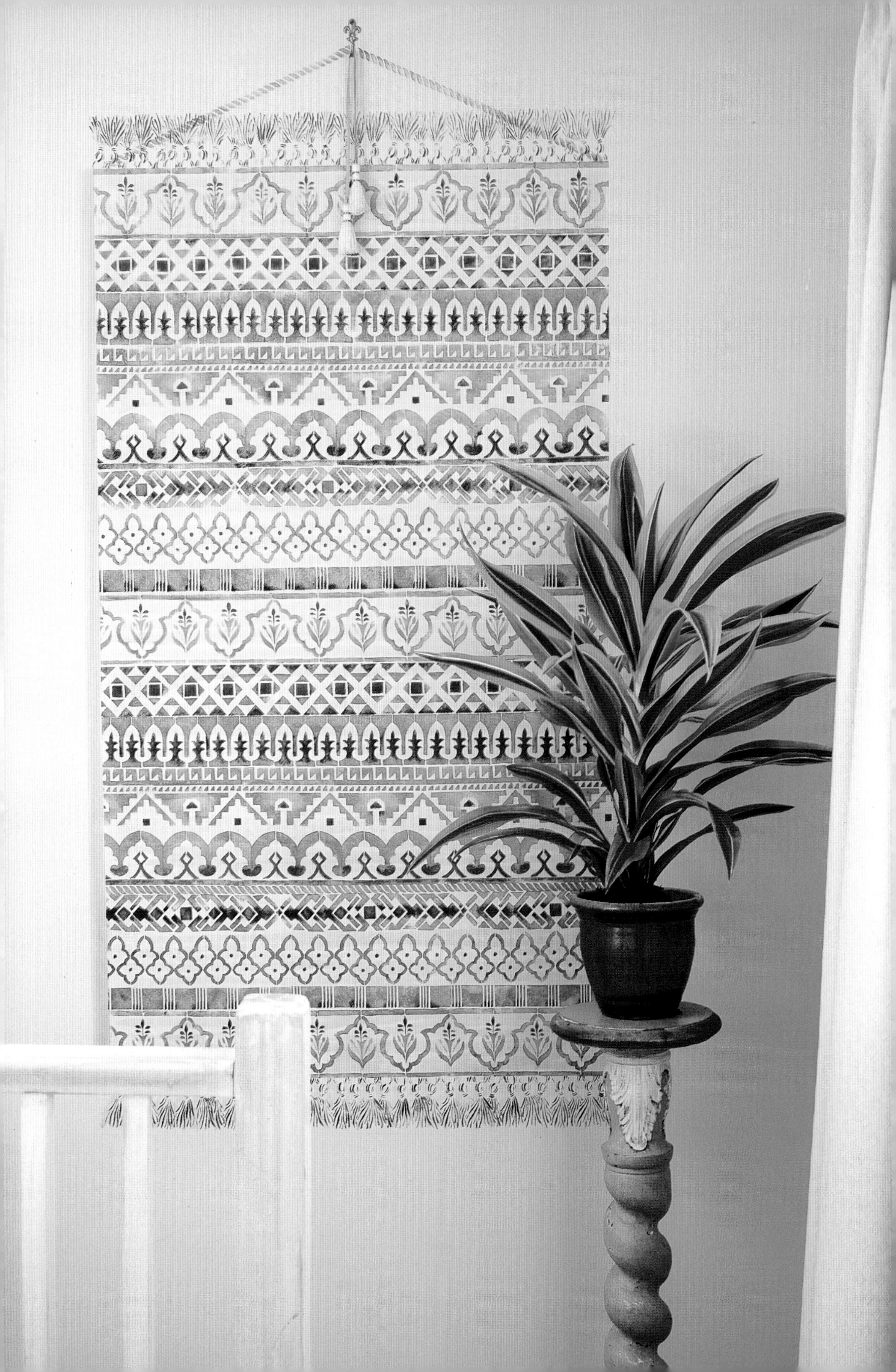

pencil
straight edge
5cm/2in wide masking tape
photocopier
acetate sheet
heat pen
glass sheet
spray adhesive
oil crayons in brown, black, copper, cherry red,
    olive green and gold
stencil brushes
brass hook and nail
hammer
artist's brush
cold tea
acrylic varnish
large paintbrush

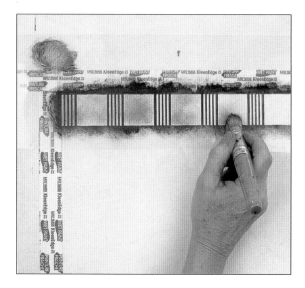

1 Select several of the kilim rug border stencils at the back of the book. Decide on the shape and size of your rug and mark it on the wall with a pencil and straight edge. Use masking tape to outline the shape. Enlarge and cut the stencils following the instructions on pages 18 and 19. Spray the edge of the reverse side of the first stencil with a light, even coat of spray adhesive and position it in the top left-hand corner of the masked area, so that it butts onto the edge of the tape. Using the blank area of the stencil (or a piece of plain paper) as a palette, rub the brown crayon onto it. Using a circular motion, pick up the colour on the stencil brush and transfer it to the cut-out area of the stencil, again pushing the brush in a circular motion. Cover one pattern in brown.

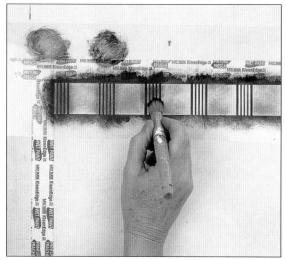

2 Repeat the process using black crayon, covering the striped area of the stencil. Overlap the brown to shade it around the edges. Overlapping colours in this way will add to the richness.

3 Position the next border stencil and colour this in copper and brown. Stencil the entire area, shading and mixing the colours as desired until the rug is covered. Remove the masking tape.

4 Using the black crayon, stencil the tasselled fringe at the top and bottom ends of the rug. Finally stencil the rope at the top, making a gentle V-shape to hang over the real brass hook. Nail the brass hook in place. Leave the work to dry for at least 48 hours.

5 With an artist's brush dipped in cold tea, make a faint narrow line to the left-hand side and at the bottom of the rug to suggest shadow. If you are not confident that you have a really steady hand, mask the two edges first and paint between the tapes. Apply an acrylic varnish to protect the rug.

Wall-to-Floor Tiles

One of the simplest projects in the book, this is also one of the most effective painted illusions known, and will transform a bathroom dramatically. It's hard to find real wall tiles that match floor tiles exactly because the quality and thickness vary between the two, but the visual advantage – a total integration of a small space – can be attained with paint. The savings, in terms of expense and the hard work of cutting and fixing tiles, are enormous.

If you like tiles with a hand-fired look, the walls need not be perfect, although textured wallpapers such as woodchip paper do need to be removed. The choice of colour combination is crucial. You may prefer to combine one colour with white, or choose a paler range of cream and white, or yellow and white, in which case the base colour needs to be a pale beige to allow the 'grouting' to show up.

For a richer, oriental look, choose a spectrum of darker colours. Use a tile size that suits your own room. A visit to your local bathroom or tile showroom may well provide the inspiration you need.

off-white vinyl silk emulsion paint
large and medium paintbrushes
cardboard
measuring tape
pencil
straight edge
scissors
5mm/¼in signwriter's tape
acrylic scumble glaze
bright blue and turquoise emulsion paint
mutton cloth
acrylic varnish
polyurethane floor varnish

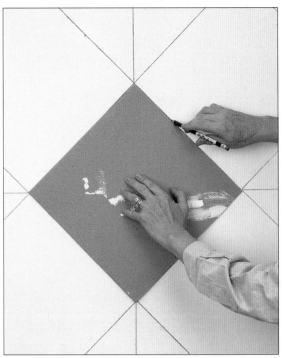

1 Paint the area to be decorated with two coats of off-white vinyl silk emulsion paint. Cut a piece of cardboard 30cm/12in square to use as a template. To find the centre of the wall, use a tape measure and rule a straight horizontal line across the middle and a vertical line through the centre. Place the cardboard template at a diagonal with one corner on the centre point and draw around it. Using the tile outline as a guide, draw long diagonal lines across the wall one way and then the other to create the diamond pattern.

2 Mask over the diagonal pencil lines with narrow signwriter's tape.

3 Add some acrylic glaze to the blue and turquoise paint. The mix should be about half-and-half to obtain the right intensity of colour. Paint the blue glaze onto the first tile using an ordinary paintbrush.

4 Using a piece of mutton cloth, gently obliterate the brush strokes. Rub the tile in the centre, to create soft highlights.

5 Paint the adjoining tile with the turquoise glaze and treat in the same way. Continue the process until the whole wall is covered and then remove the masking tape. Repeat the process for the remaining walls. Tackle the floor in exactly the same way, matching the pattern and linking the lines of grouting. Protect the walls with two coats of waterproof acrylic varnish and apply three or four coats of polyurethane floor varnish to the floor area.

Mahogany Bathroom Panelling

Victorian and Edwardian bathrooms have never really gone out of date which is why mahogany, intrinsic to their style, is an ever-popular wood-grain effect. Traditionally, real mahogany panels in bathrooms would have been teamed with dark, richly patterned nineteenth-century wallpapers: a rather gloomy combination. Today's format is altogether brighter. The classic scheme shown here is achieved with colourwashed walls in honey beige to offset the deep mahogany tones. Painted on the cupboard doors and matching bath panel, mahogany adds rich upmarket appeal which goes particularly well with real marble.

The lightest mahoganies have great reflective qualities, with yellow or pinkish hues, while the darker varieties exhibit deep red to terracotta brown shades. The finished result is determined mainly by your choice of base colour, which can vary from dusky pink nectarine to terracotta. For the most expensive-looking effect and definite grain, the terracotta seems to work best for me, but it is a matter of personal taste. Once you have mixed the right colour glaze, the actual paint effect is really simple.

MATERIALS AND EQUIPMENT

terracotta vinyl silk emulsion
paint
medium paintbrush
acrylic varnish
masking tape
acrylic scumble glaze
artist's acrylic colours in burnt
      sienna, burnt umber and
      Mars black
softening brush
stencil brush
clear wax polish or satin acrylic
varnish
cloth

1 Apply two coats of terracotta emulsion paint to cover the panelling. When dry, apply a coat of acrylic varnish to create a non-absorbent base for the glaze.

2 Mask off the central panel. Mix a dark brown glaze with the artist's acrylic colours, using equal parts of paint and glaze, and apply it to the panel using an ordinary paintbrush.

3 With the same brush, make an arch pattern in the glaze keeping it at the same angle throughout. Continue the brush stroke right to the edge of the panel. Wobble the lines towards the top of the arch in a gentle M-shape.

4 Soften across the grain using the softening brush, working lightly to blur the edges of the brush strokes and create a cloudy effect.

5 Apply the glaze to one edge of the panel at a time and, working from one side to the other, organize the wet glaze into roughly parallel bands by varying the pressure on the bristles and the angle of the brush to produce variations in tone. Aim for neat straight joints in the panelling: these can be done with masking tape if you are prepared to wait for the glaze to dry.

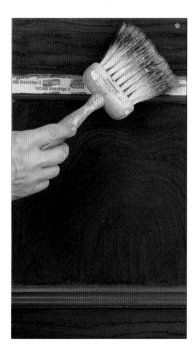

6 Soften the brush strokes with the softening brush, dragging it lightly across the stripes at an angle. Make occasional up and down strokes to confirm the direction of the grain.

7 When the glaze is dry, use a stencil brush to cover the moulding. Stipple on the glaze to give it tonal variety and to soften it as before. When thoroughly dry, apply wax or satin acrylic varnish to give the surface a patina.

China *Trompe L'Oeil* Shelf

When you can pull off a *trompe-l'oeil* trick which in real life would be a practical impossibility, you are close to topping the fakers' league tables. Nobody in their right mind would risk positioning this collection of pretty china on a shelf above a door liable to slam and shatter it. A row of painted jugs and vases, however, presents no such danger.

As a double bluff, you can position a real shelf above the door – just a narrow one – and sit a few unbreakable plastic pieces on it. Selecting mainly blue and white as a colour scheme unifies the collection and makes it stand out, especially when set against this stone colourwash. Shading the shapes before stencilling the patterns adds a three-dimensional feel, and shading behind the shapes is also important. Choose as many designs as you need to fill your shelf. The planter with tiger lilies, Chinese jar, patterned pitcher, jug with tulips and thin-necked vase used here can all be found at the back of the book or you can buy pre-cut stencils (see the suppliers list).

sand colourwash
large paintbrush
mutton cloth
photocopier
tracing paper
felt-tipped pen
acetate sheet
glass sheet
spray adhesive
masking tape
heat pen
stencil paint in white, mauve, 3–4 shades of blue,
     bright red and 2 shades of green
stencil brushes
cloth
medium artist's brush
cold tea
light brown oil crayon
small wooden shelf
brackets and screws
screwdriver

1 Colourwash the walls following the instructions on pages 16 and 17. Photocopy the stencils and cut, following the instructions on pages 18 and 19. Stick the shapes on the wall with spray adhesive, spacing them to suit the shelf width, to check that they fit and look good together. Beginning with the jug in the middle, stick the outline shape in position and stencil in white to obliterate the colourwash. Shade the right-hand side of the jug with mauve-blue paint, creating a gentle curve to suggest a rounded shape. Repeat using pale green for the left-hand side. Leave a white highlight in the middle.

2 Using a damp cloth, blend the paint to soften the edges.

3 Spray the reverse of the second layer stencil with adhesive and position accurately to line up with the shape on the wall. Stencil the design using bright red to colour the tops of the tulip petals, dark green for the leaves, mauve and blue for the flowers on the jug and pale green for the leaves on the jug. Using mainly blue and white, stencil the other shapes along the shelf, remembering to block them in first with white paint.

4 Using an artist's brush and cold tea, draw a thin line of shadow along one side and around the bottom of each stencil. The position of the shading will depend on the direction of your light source.

5 With a stencil brush and some pale brown oil crayon, shade the area to the side of each piece of china. Screw the shelf brackets and shelf in place to clip the bottom of the stencilled shapes.

Secret Door Alcove

The fashion for secret doors goes back many centuries. They led into villainous secret passages and priest-holes long before grand houses hid them in panelled walls for butlers slipping in and out of the kitchen quarters. Today, disguising a door in a room with just too many doors for visual comfort is a fun option and makes the space feel a lot cosier. It will also cheer up a cheap-looking flush door and inject colour and interest into a dull corner.

This alcove is designed to suit a cosy cottage-style kitchen, with a painted timber back, pretend shelves and a herringbone pattern to the doors – a design commonly used on farmhouse or stable doors. Proper lightweight moulding and bull's eye corner pieces frame the door, and the fake drawer is edged in real wooden moulding in a rope design. The corresponding pretend carved edge which curves around the top of the alcove is thick piping cord painted green. The knobs on the door are real. These solid additions help to cut down the work involved and pro-vide a touch of authenticity. The shelves are filled with stencils of a model duck, books and bookends, a tiger lily in a planter, glasses and a Chinese jar.

MATERIALS AND EQUIPMENT

flush door
laminate primer
medium paintbrush
vinyl silk emulsion paint in
    terracotta, off-white and
    apple green
pencil and straight edge
5mm/¼in signwriter's tape,
    2.5cm/1in masking tape and
    2.5cm/1in flexible tape
paper
pre-tinted acrylic scumble glaze
    in white, dark green-blue
    and apricot
craft knife
steel rule
wood-grainer
stencil brushes
photocopier
tracing paper
felt-tipped pen
acetate sheet
glass sheet
spray adhesive
heat pen
stencil paints
wooden mouldings
coping saw
2 bull's eye mouldings to match
    width of door frame
glue gun
panel pins (optional)
hammer (optional)
2 china knobs
thick piping cord

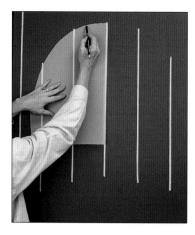

1 If the door is covered with plastic laminate, treat it with an appropriate primer so that further coats of paint will adhere. Paint with two coats of terracotta emulsion. Using a pencil and straight edge, mark the position of the door frame and cover with signwriter's tape. Rule and mask the five vertical lines for the sides and back of the alcove. Make a paper template half the shape and size of the alcove. Pencil in the curve for the alcove and flip the template to mark the other half. Mask the curved line with flexible tape.

2 Draw and mask two straight lines for the middle and two for the bottom shelves using signwriter's tape. Mask sloping lines for both sides of the top and bottom shelves, and rule and mask a line for the back of each shelf. Rule and mask an outline for the drawer, masking the position of the moulding with 2.5cm/1in tape. Draw lines and mask the herringbone pattern on the cupboard front. Paint the inside back of the alcove in off-white emulsion paint. Paint the rest in apple green.

3 When the paint is dry, use an ordinary paintbrush to apply an apricot glaze to the alcove area, working in the direction of the planks. Cover the shelves as well, using horizontal strokes, and leave to dry.

4 Remove the masking tapes around the planks and shelves, scoring along their edges first with a craft knife and a steel rule. This will ensure that none of the surrounding paint is torn away and will also create a more definite line. When all tapes have been removed, apply a white glaze in the direction of the planks.

5 While the glaze is still wet, draw a wood-grainer through it in one continuous movement, rocking it gently and working from top to bottom to create a wood-grained effect. Paint the shelf and the front edge of the shelf in the same glaze, dragging it horizontally. Repeat this process for the remaining planking below this shelf. Treat the bottom shelf in the same way, but note that the edge of the shelf should be painted in green-blue glaze.

6 With a stencil brush, stipple an extra coat of apricot glaze on the top of each shelf and onto the inside edges of the alcove, making them a shade darker to create depth. Apply a coat of green-blue glaze to the arch, drawer and door front. Score the edges of the tapes as before and lift them off.

7 Enlarge and cut the appropriate stencils at the back of the book, following the instructions on pages 18 and 19 (or buy ready-cut designs). Apply spray adhesive to the back of each stencil and position on the shelves. Stencil in off-white emulsion. Lift the stencils in turn and paint over the bridges in off-white emulsion.

8 Reposition the stencils over the white shapes and apply the appropriate colours using stencil paints and brushes. Shade the outside tips of the lilies with deep red and draw a very dry brush over the inside petals to create veins typical of tiger lilies.

9 Cut mouldings to fit around the door and drawers. Paint these and the bull's eye corner pieces in off-white emulsion and then green glaze. With a glue gun, position and stick them in place. For extra strength you can also use panel pins. Screw the china knobs onto the drawer front.

10 Cut three pieces of piping cord to fit around the curve of the alcove and paint it green. When dry, stick in position with a glue gun. Where the cord butts into the outer moulding, cut at an angle with a craft knife so that it fits neatly. Firmly glue down any frayed edges.

Sideboard Splashback

The wall behind a dining or kitchen buffet often gets dirty, which is of course why splashbacks were first invented. Painting your own allows you to evolve an individual colour scheme and tile size, and if your walls are ancient, bumpy and just not smooth enough to tile without a messy sanding job, a fake painted substitute bypasses the problem. Uneven walls actually accentuate the texture

of hand-fired tiles which you are trying to achieve.

Unlike many paint recipes for tiles this one does not require masking tape, just two simple stencils which are quick to cut and easy to apply. Finely butted up to each other, you may even find it unnecessary to paint the pretend grouting.

The design can be contained within a wooden framework made from real timber or you can paint a surrounding tile border, shaded along one side and at the bottom to create a three-dimensional effect.

MATERIALS AND EQUIPMENT

pencil
cardboard
ruler
scissors
measuring tape
masking tape
eraser
felt-tipped pen
acetate sheet
cutting mat
steel rule
craft knife
paint kettles
vinyl silk emulsion paint
      in 3 shades of green
acrylic scumble glaze
paintbrushes
mutton cloth
stippling brush
fine artist's brush
beige paint, tea or coffee
polyurethane or acrylic varnish

1 Copy and scale up the two tile patterns shown: an eight-sided tile and a small square. Cut out two cardboard templates. Find the centre of the wall behind your sideboard and rule a vertical line. Rule a starting line for the top of the splashback and mask with tape. From where these two lines cross, rule two diagonal lines down the wall to act as guidelines. Rule a straight line through the middle of the large tile and align it with the vertical line on the wall. Draw around it. Place the second tile next to it and draw around it. Repeat this process for large and small tiles until you have covered the area of the splashback. Remove the diagonal pencil guidelines with an eraser.

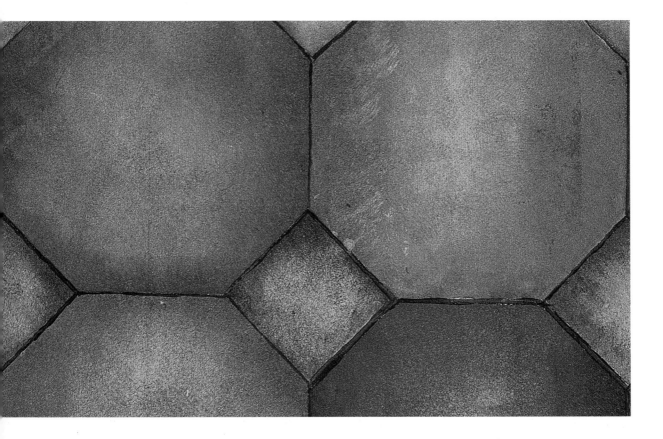

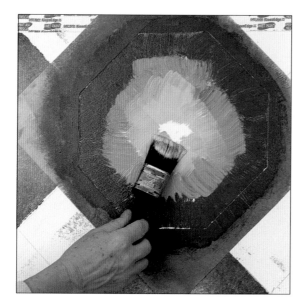
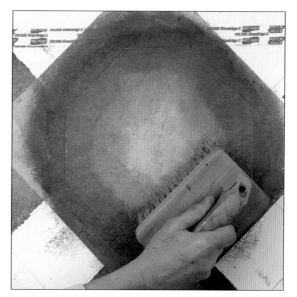

2 Using the cardboard templates, cut two acetate stencils following the instructions on pages 18 and 19. Mix three different shades of green glaze, using half paint and half scumble glaze to produce intense colours. Cover the back of the large stencil with spray adhesive and position on the wall. Apply the darkest shade of green to the tile edges. Then apply the mid-green glaze inside the dark green surround, and the pale green in the centre of the tile. Dab the tile with mutton cloth to remove all brush strokes.

3 Stipple over the tile to produce a fine speckled texture. Repeat this process covering all the tiles drawn. If necessary, work on alternate tiles, leaving a tile gap between to allow them time to dry. Leave very slender gaps between tiles, and do not worry if these are barely visible. Fit the small tile stencil over the gaps and repeat the process, omitting the mid-green. For the top, bottom and sides mask the tile stencils to create a straight edge.

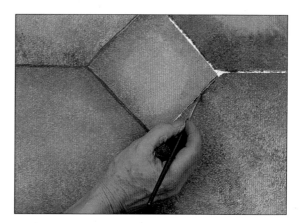

4 Using a fine artist's brush, paint narrow, dark green lines between the tiles to represent grout. If some tiles have butted into each other without leaving a gap, paint over the tiles. Tape two lines of 5mm/¼in signwriter's tape around the finished work. Mask lines across the border to break it into small, oblong tiles. Paint over this border in the same way. Remove the masking tape. Paint a pretend shadow line to one side of the tiles and along the bottom using beige paint, tea or coffee. Protect the work with varnish.

SIDEBOARD SPLASHBACK **91**

The Big Pretenders

Caribbean Seascape

The best views in the world can be faked through a pretend window, and even a simple design like this one, of a palm-fringed beach, has an uplifting effect on the viewer. Like a mirror it appears to expand space and add sparkle and, like a good painting or photograph, transports the imagination into a sunnier, warmer world. This is the most straightforward pretend window in the book, with hardly any shading and just a few stencils to cut, so it is an easy project for beginners.

The shutters are purely decorative, but you could hinge a second set to the existing pair and back them all with mirror, so that when closed the 'window' would turn into a large mirror. Above a sofa bed this is particularly useful if you want to use the room as a spare bedroom.

90 x 60cm/3 x 2ft MDF board
emulsion paint in off-white,
    bright red, 2 tones of
    yellow and mid-blue
paintbrush
pencil
ruler
small plate
2.5cm/1in flexible and straight
    masking tape
craft knife
acrylic scumble glaze
teaspoon
mutton cloth
artist's brush
wood-grainer
photocopier
tracing paper
felt-tipped pen
acetate sheet
glass sheet
spray adhesive
heat pen
stencil paints in turquoise,
    green, brown, red and blue
stencil brushes
acrylic varnish
shelf and 2 hinged shutters
screws and screwdriver

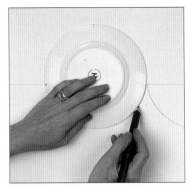

1 Paint the MDF board in off-white emulsion paint and leave to dry. Using the photograph overleaf as a guide, draw the horizon, the bottom of the awning, the windowsill and the beaches. Using a small plate as a template, divide the awning line into equal parts and draw the scallop shapes along the edge, beginning in the centre. If the scallops do not fit exactly, draw fractions of the half-circle to fill the outer edges.

2 Draw the awning stripes in pencil. Mask the scallops with flexible tape, using a craft knife to shape the ends. Add 1tsp glaze to 5tsp red paint. Using an ordinary paintbrush, paint alternate stripes in red. Leave highlights in the middle of the stripes and make the scallop shapes slightly darker by applying the glaze more thickly. Leave to dry.

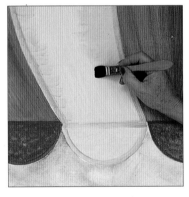

3 Add glaze to bright yellow paint in the same proportion and colour in the remaining stripes. Leave to dry. Using flexible tape, mask around the beaches. Add 1/2tsp glaze to about 5tsp blue paint and apply to the sea area in horizontal strokes. Intensify the colour along the horizon, and lighten it towards the beach by dabbing away some of the glaze with mutton cloth. For definition, add second coats of red and yellow to the creases of the awning.

4 Use a small artist's brush to create a 'hemline' along the bottom of the awning. Mask the top and bottom edge of the shelf and mix a sandy-coloured glaze to apply over the shelf area. Draw a wood-grainer through the glaze in one continuous movement, rocking it gently. When dry, remove the masking tape. Reposition the tapes to mask the beaches. Paint with a pale yellow glaze and leave to dry.

5 Remask the scalloped edge of the awning and mask the sea area to paint the sky. Apply a pale blue glaze all over the area, then mutton cloth to produce an even, cloudless sky.

6 Enlarge and cut the yucca, palm trees, bowl, cocktail glasses, umbrellas and yacht stencils at the back of the book. Apply spray adhesive to the reverse side of the glass stencil and position. Apply the off-white over the stencil and lift off. Fill in the bridges with an artist's brush.

7 Replace the glass stencil and apply turquoise paint in horizontal strokes, slightly curving them to correspond with the curve in the glass.

8 Do not make the paint on the glass too solid and leave a highlight along the shape's right-hand edge.

9 Continue this process, positioning the other stencils following the picture. Work on the small shapes first, such as the yacht and palm trees, leaving larger foreground shapes until last.

10 For the furthest palm trees, add a tiny bit of white to the paint so they appear to recede. Stencil in the yucca plant, bowl, and umbrellas in strong, clear colours. Protect the work with a coat of acrylic varnish, and position on the wall with the shelf below and shutters hinged to either side.

Landscape View from a Cottage Window

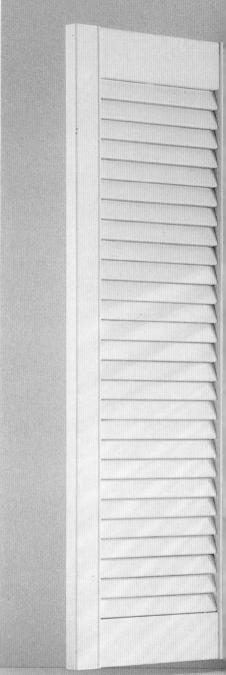

In a windowless kitchen, loo or bathroom, a simple way to relieve a feeling of claustrophobia and give an illusion of space is to install a false window. Skilfully lit and positioned, it can help to satisfy that universal craving for a peaceful view of undulating countryside which you wish would greet you every morning as you stand at the kitchen sink.

All the really difficult *trompe-l'oeil* work has been taken out of this project by using a real window and shutters to frame what is essentially a naïvely painted background, so simple a child could paint it. The stencilled motifs superimposed on the view produce the key elements in the design and guarantee the professional-looking end result, so don't give up halfway through. As with all artistic endeavours, it's the final touches that bring it all together.

MDF cut to fit inside window
    frame
medium paintbrush
off-white emulsion paint
graph paper
pencil
tracing paper
carbon paper
straight edge
flexible and straight masking
    tape
stencil paints in white, sky blue,
    3 shades of green, dark
    blue, 3 shades of brown,
    pink, red, terracotta and
    black
acrylic scumble glaze
mutton cloth
natural sponge
stencil brushes
photocopier
felt-tipped pen
acetate sheet
glass sheet
spray adhesive
heat pen
fine artist's brush
clear acrylic, waterproof varnish
window frame, painted
louvred shutters, painted to
    match frame
hinges
screws and screwdriver

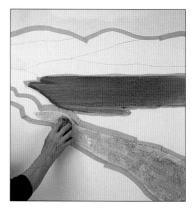

1 Paint the MDF with two coats of off-white emulsion paint and leave to dry. Draw the outlines of the landscape on graph paper following the photograph, then scale it up by drawing a grid on tracing paper to fit the window. Then transfer the design. Using carbon paper, trace the drawing onto the board. Rule a straight line for the windowsill. Using flexible tape, mask the top line of hills to separate them from the sky. Mask the lines around the lake and the path.

2 Mix a pale blue glaze and apply it to the sky. Then, with mutton cloth, dab over the area to eradicate brush marks and create a smooth, translucent effect. Refold the cloth to make a clean pad and, with a circular action, remove the blue glaze to leave a line of interlocking, billowing, round white cloud shapes. Add highlights to the top left-hand edge of each cloud by dabbing with a stencil brush loaded with white stencil paint. Mix a dark blue glaze for the lake and apply with horizontal parallel strokes to create a flat, watery effect. Make sure you extend the brush to the edges of the lake. Mix three different shades of brown and use the palest to fill in the path. With a sponge, dab on the remaining browns to make a speckled, pebbly texture.

3 Once these areas have dried, mix a pale green glaze for the furthest hill. Mask the shape and apply the glaze with a stencil brush. Dab the glaze with mutton cloth as before to remove brush marks. Mask off the windowsill and paint in a sandy colour. Stand back to view the work and add a second green glaze to the lake to soften and intensify the watery effect. Remember that water furthest away looks denser and darker, so, if necessary, apply a second coat of blue to accentuate the lake's horizon. Add a small amount of darker green to the glaze used for the first hill, mask around the central hill and paint as before. Treat the remaining hillside in the same way, increasing the intensity of colour as you advance towards the foreground. For the grassy bank nearest to the windowsill, use several shades of green, stippled over the surface with a small stencil brush to create a grassy texture.

4 Enlarge and cut the stencils at the back of the book. Stencil the tree shapes using mid-green for the leaves and branches, and mid-brown for the trunks. Place the larger trees along the edge of the lake and mask the bottom of the trunks so that they line up with the waterline. Place the smaller trees furthest away, and mask the trunks so that they appear to be sitting on the brow of the hill.

5 Using spray adhesive, stick the remaining stencils in position and paint the cat, ducks, planter, daisy plant and auricula pots using a stencil brush and white paint.

6 Remove the stencils and use a fine artist's brush to paint over the gaps left 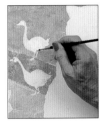 by the stencil bridges so that the shapes are blocked in white. Apply a second coat of white emulsion – and, if necessary, a third – until all the background colours are obliterated.

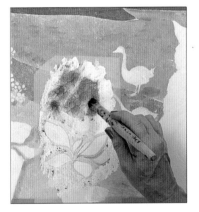

7 With a very pale brown glaze and a fine artist's brush, shade the bottom right and base of the stencil outlines positioned along the windowsill. Shade lightly along the water's edge, between the lines of the hills and under the ducks.

8 Stencil in the remaining shapes using the appropriate colours. The objects closest to the eye should appear brightest in the picture. If necessary, you can intensify colours like the red of the auricula by applying a second coat of paint.

9 Shape the pots by leaving white highlights and curving your brush strokes. Mix a dark green with which to stencil the leaves around the top and sides of the window. This should be the densest of all, so the leaves and berries look as though they are growing on the outside wall. Protect the work with clear acrylic varnish. Attach hinges to the shutters and screw to either side of the frame. Position the painted scene behind the frame and fix to the wall.

Tuscan Landscape

This painted illusion on cupboard doors is a perfect space-expanding trick for a cramped landing or the end of a narrow, featureless hall. Sensibly enough, alcoves tend to be taken over for built-in storage, so why not combine the convenience of an extra cupboard with the working out of a fantasy? And who could resist the allure of an ornate balcony with a pretty view over verdant Tuscan hills, particularly if it can be painted without special artistic skills?

This fake view was painted onto plain flush doors, but the design could be adapted to fit into a panelled door. The wooden moulding cut to frame each door, the real handles and the white louvred shutters are visually important ingredients which help to authenticate the fake – and in this case the shutters hide a rather ugly wall-hung telephone. As with all successful mural cheats, there are rules to help you succeed, so before picking up a paintbrush, see pages 8 and 9 for some useful reminders. Although this project may look daunting, broken down into simple stages it really is easy and rewarding.

MATERIALS AND EQUIPMENT

white vinyl silk emulsion paint
medium paintbrush
coping saw
thin, flat moulding
pencil
straight edge
2.5cm/1in masking tape,
    flexible tape and
    5mm/¼in signwriter's tape
photocopier
tracing paper
felt-tipped pen
acetate sheet
glass sheet
spray adhesive
heat pen
emulsion paint in a selection of
    colours
acrylic scumble glaze
mutton cloth
small roller and paint tray
natural sponge
panel pins
hammer
acrylic varnish
hinged, louvred shutters
screws
screwdriver

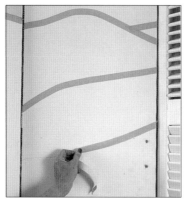

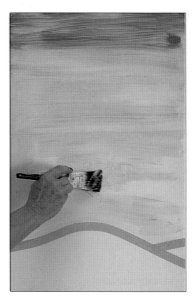

1 Apply two coats of white vinyl silk emulsion paint to the cupboard doors. Saw and mitre lengths of flat moulding to create a frame for each door. Do not attach them yet. Rule and mask a line for the quarry-tiled floor, and mark the positions for the top and bottom of the balcony stencil. Using the photographs for reference, pencil in the lines of hills. Mask the outline shapes for the hills with flexible tape. Enlarge and cut the stencils for the balcony, cypress trees, farmhouse, peach tree and leaves, following the instructions on pages 18 and 19.

2 Mix a blue glaze and apply in horizontal brush strokes to cover the sky area. Add an extra dollop of blue to make the top of the sky darkest, and lighten it as you move down towards the hill line.

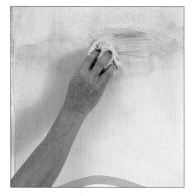

3 With a piece of mutton cloth, dab over this area to eradicate brush strokes. Mutton cloth the area just behind the hilltops more vigorously to create a paler sky.

4 Cover the floor area with buff-coloured emulsion paint using a small roller and paint tray. When dry, mask the pattern for the floor tiles with narrow signwriter's tape, taking the perspective into account.

5 Using the same paint roller, go over the floor area with deep terracotta, working the roller patchily to give the tiles a hand-fired look. When the floor is dry, mask off the meadow in the foreground and use a natural sponge to apply several different tones of green to create a grass texture.

6 When dry, apply a sponge dipped in red and yellow to create a pattern of tiny flower heads. When dry, remask the meadow and apply a paler green glaze to cover the hill beyond it. Leave to dry, then stencil the balcony fence panels in black. With panel pins and a hammer, fix the ready-cut mouldings to frame the two doors.

7 Remask the remaining hills, and with a paler green glaze and natural sponge apply different tones of green, making sure they become increasingly pale in the distance.

8 Position the tree group stencil along the curve of the hill, and mask off the bottoms of the trunks to fit them into the hill line. Reverse the tree stencil and apply to the opposite door. Stencil in the smaller lines of trees and finally the Tuscan farmhouse, masking the shape to fit the curve of the hill as before.

9 Stencil the trees in two shades of green, making one side darker to give a three-dimensional effect.

10 Position the peach branches so they appear to belong to a tree growing up the left-hand side of the window. Use colours that blend with the landscape. Highlight the peaches in yellow and shade in apricot. Position and stencil the remaining branches.

11 Using dark green mixed with black, position and stencil the leaves to cascade in front of, and frame the view. These should extend almost to the top of the balcony in a random, natural pattern. Halve some of the leaf stencils with masking tape, so only a few leaves project into the picture. Paint the moulding around the door white and apply a coat of acrylic varnish to protect the painting. Screw the louvred shutters in place on the cupboard door frame.

Greek Island Balcony

A folding screen makes a perfect canvas for mural painting since, unlike a scene painted directly onto the wall, you can take it with you when you move. A screen can hide away an office desk from the rest of the sitting room, or conceal the kitchen clutter and envelope a romantic cosy place for a dining table at the same time. Best of all, you can determine your own escapist view by what you paint. This Greek island scene of a balcony overlooking the Aegean Sea is a reminder of many summer holidays and is much simpler to create than it may appear.

Tackling a large canvas is less daunting and easier to arrange when it is divided into four screen sections. When you analyse the ingredients, there are only three main background areas to paint – the paving stones, sea and sky – and they can easily be drawn with a straight edge. The trellis and mountains are both done with masking tape and the rest of the scene requires just five

stencils. In many ways seascapes call for less artistic skill than landscapes, so you could argue that this is one of the easiest mural scenes in the book. To cut down the work of cutting stencils, you could use flexible masking tape to paint the arch, and to avoid having to cut out stencils altogether, the list of sources for ready-cut designs is at the back of the book.

MDF folding screen, 1.5 x 2m/5 x 6½ft
white vinyl silk emulsion paint
medium paintbrush
pencil
straight edge
1cm/½in and 2.5cm/1in masking tape and
    flexible tape
emulsion or acrylic paint in grey, mid-blue,
    orange, bright yellow, turquoise and white
acrylic scumble glaze to mix with sky blue and
    pale yellow artist's acrylics
mutton cloth
small roller and paint tray
photocopier
tracing paper
felt-tipped pen
acetate sheet
glass sheet

spray adhesive
heat pen
artist's brush
oil crayons in gold, brown, black, green, red and
    terracotta
stencil brushes
acrylic varnish

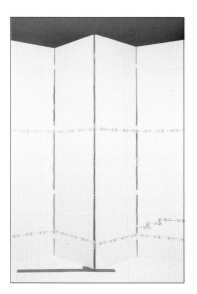

1 Paint the screen with two coats of white vinyl silk emulsion paint. With a pencil and straight edge, draw and then mask off horizontal lines to define the position of the horizon and the top of the paving stones which edge the balcony floor. Draw and mask the steps leading from the balcony to the beach, using the photograph as a guide to their position.

2 Paint the paving-stone area in one coat of grey emulsion paint. Paint a band of pale blue glaze at the top of the sky area and paint a band of yellow glaze along the horizon. Blend the two areas using mutton cloth. Concentrate the darkest blue towards the top of the sky, applying a second coat of blue glaze if necessary. Make sure the sky is much lighter at the bottom.

3 When the paint is dry, reposition the masking tape in order to enclose the sea area. Add some glaze to some mid-blue emulsion paint and with an ordinary paintbrush apply it in horizontal strokes. Paint over the area nearest the horizon several times to intensify the colour. Thin the glaze and apply to the seashore area, blending the colours in between. Make sure this area is much lighter in texture and colour.

4 Add some glaze to a blob of orange paint and apply to the sky with a stencil brush in long thin splodges. Soften the effect to create elongated sunset clouds. Repeat the process using a bright yellow glaze.

5 Mix a small amount of glaze with some turquoise paint, and with an ordinary paintbrush move horizontally across the sea area to add bright patches of turquoise to match as nearly as possible the colour of sandy patches at the bottom of the Mediterranean. Concentrate the turquoise in the sea area nearest the beach as well, but avoid the horizon. This needs to be the deepest blue on the screen.

6 With pencil and straight edge, draw the paving-stone lines onto the grey area at the bottom of the screen. Use the photograph as a guide for this. With a small roller and paint tray, go over the paved area patchily to create texture, allowing some of the grey to show through. Remove the masking tape.

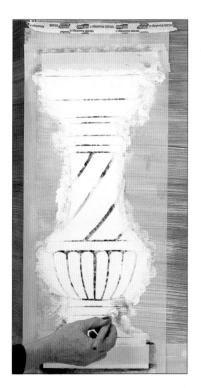

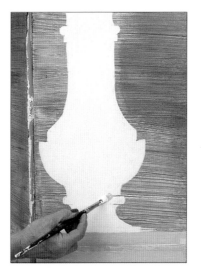

7 Enlarge and cut the stencils at the back of the book for the balustrade, geranium in a pot, auricula pots, flower and leaf and wrought-iron half-arch, following the instructions on pages 18 and 19. Carefully position the first balustrade stencil with spray adhesive and stencil in white.

8 Remove the stencil. Using an artist's brush, go over the bridges around the edges, and use a larger brush to go over the centre of the outline to create a solid white shape. You may need to repeat the process several times to remove all signs of blue and turquoise paint.

9 Reposition the balustrade stencil and go over the right-hand side of it with gold crayon and the left-hand side with mid-brown. This will lighten the area where the sun is falling. Shade the rest of the stencil, leaving highlights between bridges to give solidity.

10 Remove the stencil and reposition it next to the one just completed. Work along the screen until you have positioned five balustrade stencils in the same way. Mask off the bottom and top of the same stencil and reposition to the extreme right of the screen on the edge of the first step leading down to the sea. Stencil it to match the others.

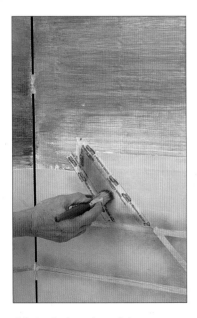

11 Mask the edge of the steps leading down to the sea and shade with brown oil crayon using a stencil brush.

12 Draw two hills along the horizon following the photograph. Apply flexible masking tape around the nearest hill. Mix a small amount of blue glaze with orange to make a pale mauve glaze. Apply with a brush and then dab with a mutton cloth to soften. Remask the adjoining hill and repeat the process.

13 Position the wrought-iron half-arch stencil so the top of the arch sits a short distance from the top of the screen. Make sure it is vertical and parallel with the side of the screen. Fix securely with spray adhesive. Go over the shape with a black oil crayon and stencil brush. Remove and reverse the stencil. Position to match the one just stencilled, butting the top curves together. Stencil as before. Repeat for the second arch. To complete the shape, attach the wrought-iron straight piece to the bottom of the arch and stencil in black crayon as before. To soften the effect, go over the arches with white glaze to create a softer, shaded grey.

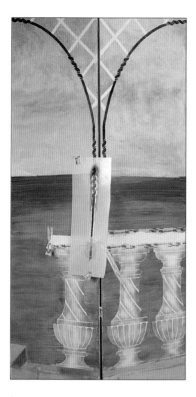

14 Using a straight edge and pencil, draw lines to outline the trellis. Mask over the pencil lines with 1cm/½in masking tape. Place masking tape on either side of this tape. Remove the middle tape and paint in white. You may need two coats. Work on the trellis pieces running parallel in one direction then repeat the process for the pieces crossing in the opposite direction. Mask a 2.5cm/1in wide band along the top of the balustrading. Paint in white and when dry use a stencil brush and crayon to match the colour of the balustrading. This will create a shelf for pots.

15 Where the trellis crosses, mask a square U-shape, and stencil a 1cm/½in square area with the brown oil crayon. Do this consistently below each crossing point on the bottom right-hand side to make shadows.

16 Apply the flower and leaf stencils to the trellis. To make it look as though some leaves are growing behind the trellis, once you have stencilled the shapes in white simply mask over some of the appropriate sections of trellis, where the leaves and flowers cross it, before applying the colours.

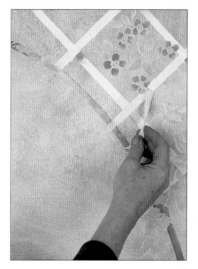

17 Apply the green and red crayons, and lift off the tape. You will have blocked off part of a leaf so it appears to be growing behind the trellis.

18 Stencil the terracotta pots and plants in the same way, creating a white background first. Finally, with the same grey paint used initially for the paving-stone base colour, paint the shadows on the paving, one for each balustrade. Varnish the screen to protect your work.

Orchard and Arches Mural

Although painting a mural onto a blank wall may seem daunting, this project is no more difficult to execute than the smaller window designs in this book. The important considerations are whether you can muster the energy to attempt it, and how to integrate existing features like doors and windows.

In this attic sitting room, the centrally placed arched window, which initially posed the problem of how to make visual sense of it, provided key inspiration. As a window could not appear to 'float' in a landscape, it needed to be set in a wall. This in turn needed to be integrated with the rest of the room, so the idea of creating two more arched openings on either side of the window took shape.

Because the real life view is from a third floor window looking down over treetops, the painted view had to echo the same bird's eye angle. The low walls at the bottom of each opening play a vital part in preventing vertigo, but in a ground floor room you could leave these out and create an illusion of immediate access into a grassy meadow. To fill the empty space above the real window, a pretend bull's eye window has leaves stencilled around it to match the foliage in the real window.

off-white vinyl silk emulsion
   paint
large and medium paintbrushes
pencil and graph paper
measuring tape
straight edge
2.5cm/1in masking tape and
   flexible tape
emulsion paints in pale blue,
   3 shades of green and mauve
acrylic scumble glaze
mutton cloth
photocopier
tracing paper
felt-tipped pen
acetate sheet
glass sheet
spray adhesive
heat pen
stencil paints in brown, green,
   red, yellow, blue, beige,
   grey and black
stencil and artist's brushes
natural sponge
acrylic varnish

1 Paint the walls of the room with two coats of off-white vinyl silk emulsion paint. Draw the main outline of your mural on a piece of graph paper and scale it to fit the size of your wall. Translate the drawing onto the wall in pencil with the help of a measuring tape. Rule the straight lines and draw the curved lines freehand, using the drawing shown in this book if applicable. With flexible tape for curves and ordinary masking tape for straight lines, mask the position and shape of the bull's eye window, arched openings, mountain ranges and lines of hills.

2 Mix some pale blue paint with acrylic scumble glaze (about half-and-half) and apply to the sky areas with an ordinary paintbrush. While the glaze is still wet, dab over with mutton cloth to create a smooth, fine texture like a sky on a clear summer's day.

3 Mix some pale green paint with acrylic scumble glaze (about half-and-half). Apply in the same way to create the distant hills below the mountain range.

4 When dry, remask the area around the mountains in order to paint and mutton cloth them in pale mauve. Mix the same quantity of paint to scumble glaze and treat in the same way. If you want to create the impression of there being immediate access into meadows, draw and mask a gentle slope in the foreground. Paint the area with a bright yellow green, dabbing the brush at an angle to create the idea of grass.

5 Fill in the remaining hillside with a darker green, mixed with a small amount of scumble glaze (about 5:1). Using an ordinary paintbrush, apply in vertical strokes at a slight angle to create the impression of long grass. Make sure the texture softens into the distance. Enlarge and cut the following stencils from the back of the book: three peach tree branch designs, tree trunk, grasses, auriculas in pots, cypress trees, bowl, trailing leaves, trellis planter, urn on a stand, butterfly, snail and grasshopper. Start with the tree. Decide whether you want to place the trunk at the bottom edge of the mural or whether you need a low wall to enclose the landscape beyond.

8 With a pencil and straight edge, rule and mask the stonework using 2.5cm/1in masking tape. Size the blocks to look like natural stone. Draw lines for the low walls if required. Using a natural sponge, sponge on different colours of grey, beige and brown to create the variety of real stonework. Concentrate the sponge effect near to the masking tape and leave areas in the middle of the blocks untouched to create highlights. Continue the stonework around the bull's eye window and across the low walls below the arched openings.

6 With the pencil, draw a rough outline of the tree, deciding where to place the branches. For the branches use brown, for leaves use shades of green, and stencil the peaches in red with a touch of yellow.

7 Every now and then, stencil a butterfly or dragonfly onto a strategic branch.

9 Remove the masking tape and leave to dry.

12 With a natural sponge dipped in white emulsion paint, go over the area again to create a softer speckled texture. Repeat this process to create depth in the top of the arched openings.

10 Using flexible tape, remask the circular frame of the bull's eye window. Draw straight lines across the frame to create the individual stones shaped to surround the window. Sponge on the paint to match the stonework.

11 Remove the masking tape. Draw an elliptical shape inside the top of the circular window to create depth. Mask the shape and with a stencil brush, colour the area in dark brown.

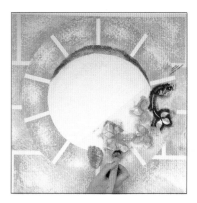

13 Apply spray adhesive to the reverse side of the leaf stencil and position to encircle the fake bull's eye window. Stencil the shape using two shades of green.

14 Build up more greenery by repositioning the same stencil, reversing it for variety.

15 With two horizontal lines of masking tape set about 5cm/2in apart, mask a ledge along the top of both low stone walls. With a stencil brush, fill in between the tapes in deep brown.

16 Position the urn stencil to sit on top of the ledge. Stencil first in white. Remove the stencil and with an artist's brush go over the bridges to make a solid white outline shape.

17 Reposition the stencil and colour in brown, leaving some central areas untouched to create shape. Continue this process, stencilling other planters and pots along the windowsills.

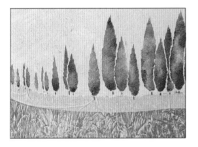

18 Using the cypress tree stencil in three different sizes, position a line of trees along the edge of the meadow. Start with the largest size, then stencil the middle size trees and reserve the smallest trees for the most distant point.

20 Remove the final stencil and protect the finished work with a coat of acrylic varnish.

19 Along the edge of the wall, stencil a line of grasses using dark green and a touch of black. Remember that shapes nearest to the eye should be the brightest and most definite.

Trace-off motifs

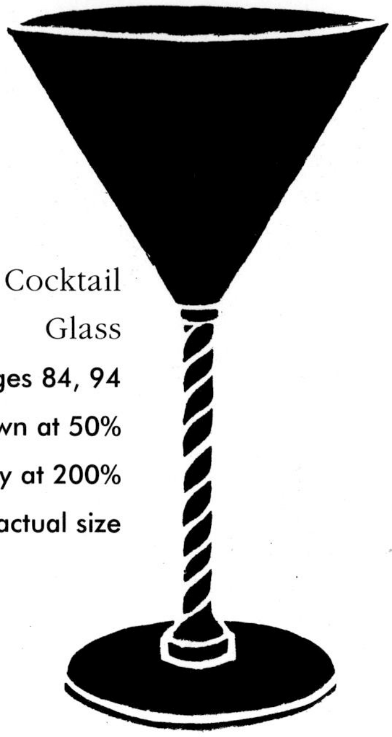

Cocktail
Glass
pages 84, 94
shown at 50%
photocopy at 200%
for actual size

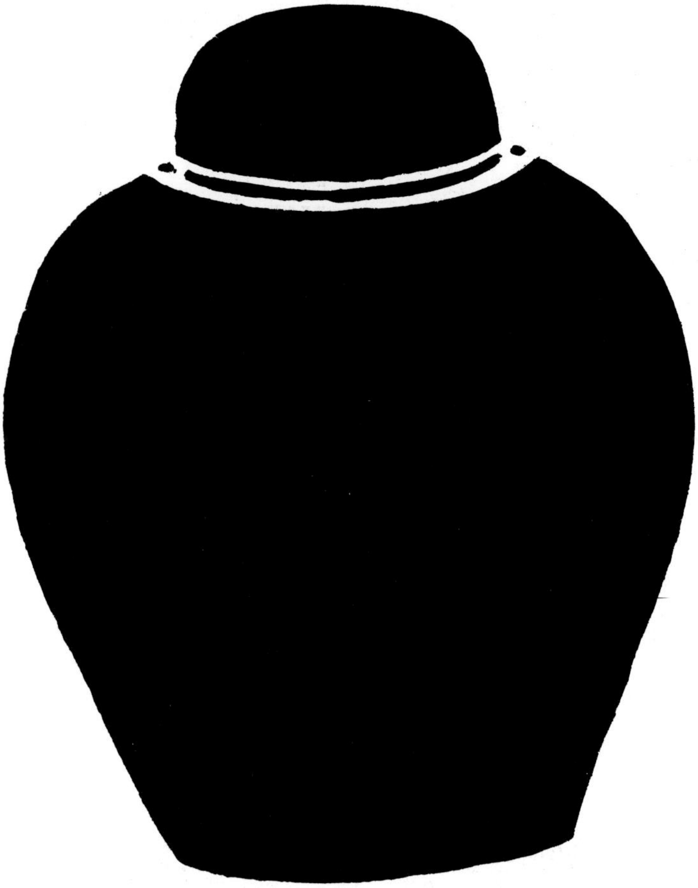

Chinese jar (layer 1)
pages 80, 84, shown at 50%
photocopy at 200% for actual size

Model duck
page 84, shown at 50%
photocopy at 200% for actual
size

Chinese jar (layer 2)
pages 80, 84
shown at 50%
photocopy at 200% for
actual size

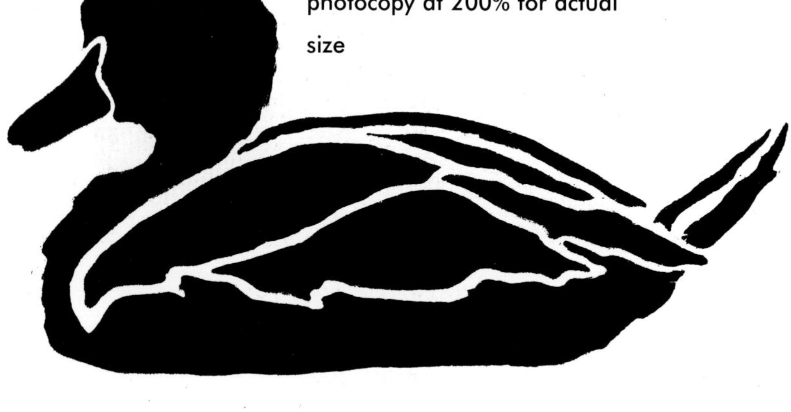

Urn on a stand
page 112, shown at 50%
photocopy at 200% for
actual size

Balustrade page 106
shown at 35%, photocopy at 285% for
actual size

Yucca plant

page 94

shown at 50%

photocopy at 200% for actual size

Tiger lilies
pages 80, 84
shown at 50%
photocopy at 200%
for actual size

Small trellis planter (layer 1)
page 80, shown at 50%, photocopy at 200% for
actual size

Small trellis planter (layer 2)
page 80, shown at 50%, photocopy at 200% for
actual size

Bowl on a stem
pages 94, 112
shown at 50%, photocopy
at 200% for actual size

Trellis pattern planter
pages 94, 112, shown at 50%,
photocopy at 200% for actual size

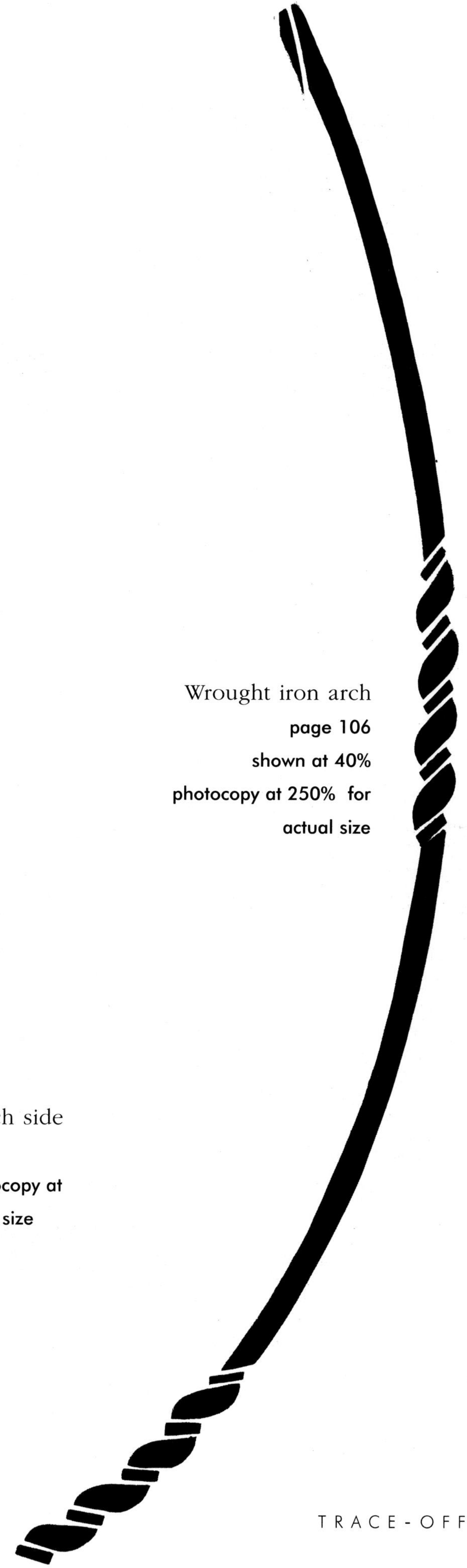

Wrought iron arch
page 106
shown at 40%
photocopy at 250% for
actual size

Wrought iron arch side
page 106
shown at 40% photocopy at
250% for actual size

Iron bedhead
page 64
shown at 40%
photocopy at 250%
for actual size

Iron bedhead **page 64**
and Balcony **page 102**
shown at 40%
photocopy at 250% for
actual size

Palm trees
page 94
shown at 50%
photocopy at 200%
for actual size

Yacht
page 94
shown at 50%
photocopy at 200%
for actual size

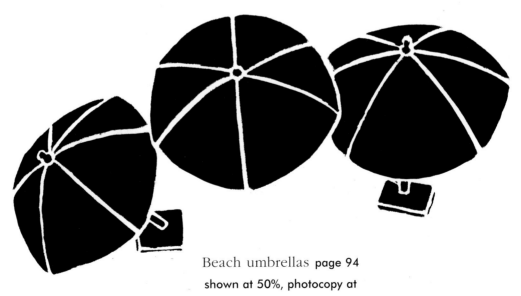

Beach umbrellas page 94
shown at 50%, photocopy at
200% for actual size

Bookends (layer 2)
page 84, shown at 50%
photocopy at 200% for
actual size

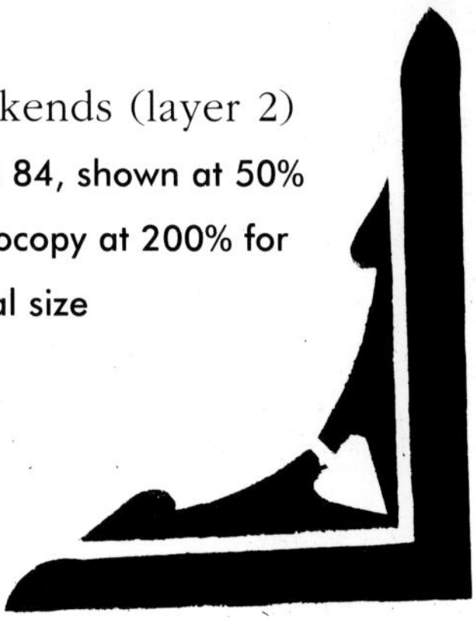

Books (layer 1)
page 84, shown at 50%
photocopy at 200% for
actual size

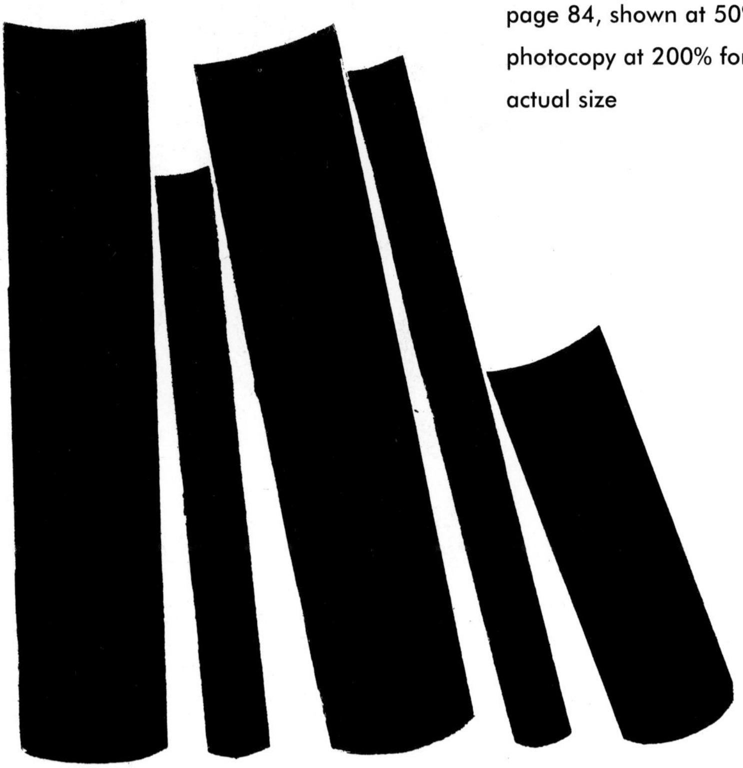

Bookends (layer 1)
page 84, shown at 50%
photocopy at 200% for
actual size

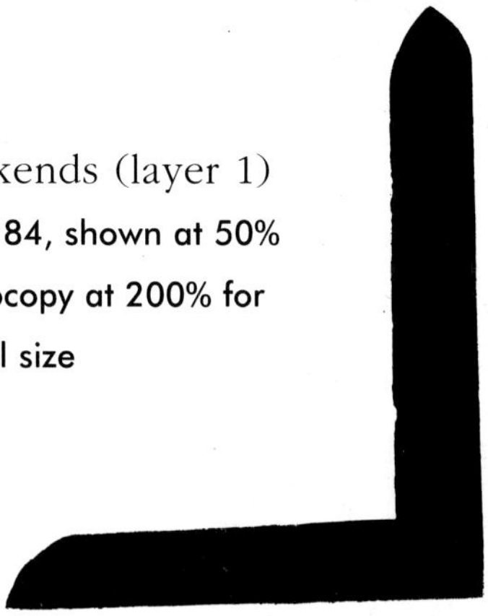

Books (layer 2)
page 84, shown at 50%
photocopy at 200% for
actual size

Kilim rug
page 68, shown at 40%
photocopy at 250% for
actual size

Indian vase
(layer 1)
page 80
shown at 50%
photocopy at 200%
for actual size

Indian vase (layer 2)
page 80, shown at 50%
photocopy at 200%
for actual size

Indian vase (layer 3)
page 80
shown at 50%
photocopy at 200%
for actual size

Tulip jug (layer 1)
page 80
shown at 50%
photocopy at 200%
for actual size

Tulip jug (layer 2)
page 80
shown at 50%
photocopy at 200%
for actual size

Antique jug (layer 1)

page 80

shown at 50%

photocopy at 200%

for actual size

Antique jug (layer 2)

page 80

shown at 50%

photocopy at 200%

for actual size

Antique jug (layer 3)

page 80

shown at 50%

photocopy at 200%

for actual size

Auricula plants in pot 1
pages 98, 106, 112
shown at 50%, photocopy at 200%
for actual size

Auricula plants in pot 2
pages 98, 106, 112
shown at 50%, photocopy at 200%
for actual size

Tuscan farmhouse
page 102, shown at 50%
photocopy at 200%
for actual size

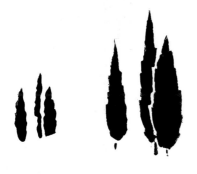

Cypress trees
pages 102, 112, shown at 50%
photocopy at 200%
for actual size

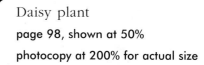

Daisy plant
page 98, shown at 50%
photocopy at 200% for actual size

Peach tree branches
pages 102 and 112
shown at 50%
photocopy at 200%
for actual size

Waddling ducks
page 98, shown at 50%
photocopy at 200%
for actual size

Ginger cat (layer 1)
page 98, shown at 50%
photocopy at 200% for actual si:

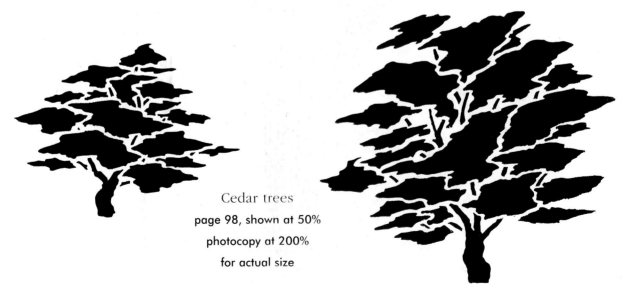

Cedar trees
page 98, shown at 50%
photocopy at 200%
for actual size

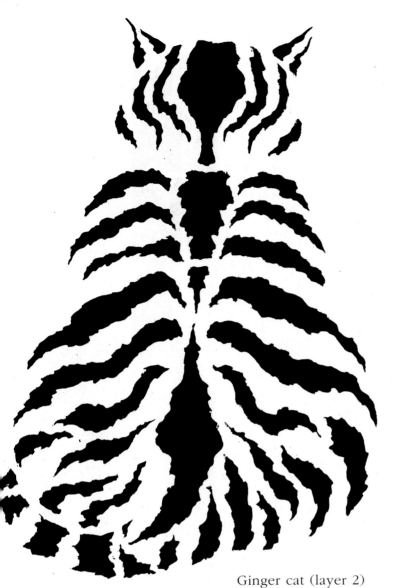

Ginger cat (layer 2)
page 98
shown at 50%
photocopy at 200%
for actual size

Leaves and berries
pages 98, 112, shown at 50%
photocopy at 200%
for actual size

Daisies
page 98, shown at 50%
photocopy at 200%
for actual size

Leaves
page 102, shown at 50%
photocopy at 200%
for actual size

Mosaic floor

page 54

shown at 40%, photocopy at

250% for actual size

Fish border (layer 1)

page 54, shown at 50%

photocopy at 200% for actual size

Fish border (layer 2)

page 54, shown at 50%

photocopy at 200% for actual size

Fish corner (layer 2)

page 54, shown at 50%

photocopy at 200% for actual size

Fish corner (layer 1)

page 54, shown at 50%

photocopy at 200% for actual size

Ivy leaves
page 102
shown at 70%
photocopy at 143%
for actual size

Flowering climber 2
page 106, shown at 70%
photocopy at 143% for
actual size

Flowering climber 1
page 106
shown at 70%
photocopy at 143% for
actual size

Small geranium he
page 106
actual size

Flower pot
page 106
actual size

Large geranium head
page 106
actual size

Geranium leaves
page 106, shown at 80%
photocopy at 125% for
actual size

Orchard insects
page 113
actual size

Suppliers

BLANKS TO PAINT
Dormy House
Stirling Park
East Portway Industrial Estate
Andover
Hampshire SP10 3TZ
Tel: 01264 365808
(screen, page 106)

Scumble Goosie
Lewiston Mill
Toadsmoor Road
Stroud
Gloucestershire G15 2TB
Tel: 01453 731305
(hall table, page 28;
side table, page 88)

FLOORS
Lecaflor Carpets
Unit 1
Beza Road
Leeds LS10 2BR
Tel: 0113 2775 776
(page 76)

Pergo Floor
Perstrop Flooring UK
Unit 14
Silver Jubilee Way
Hazlemere Heathrow Industrial
Estate
Heathrow TW3 6NF
Tel: 0181 754 1777
(page 113)

FURNITURE AND ACCESSORIES
Cargo Homeshop
Whiteleys of Bayswater
Queensway Road
London W2
(table, page 25; bathroom
accessories, page 54)

Christy
PO Box 19, Newton Street
Hyde
Cheshire SK14 4N7
Tel: 0161 954 9322
(towels)

Croft and Assinder
Standard Brassworks
Lombard Street
Digbath
Birmingham B12 OQX
Tel: 0121 622 1074
(kitchen handles, page 59)

Elephant Furniture
169-171 Queensway
London W2 4SB
Tel: 0171 467 0630
(candlesticks, pages 29 and 50;
tables, pages 41 and 45; chairs,
pages 65, 77 and 113; plant
stand, page 69)

Evergreen Trading
12 Martindale
East Sheen
London SW14 7AL
Tel: 0181 878 4050
(accessories, page 89)

Hayloft
3 Bond Street
Chiswick
London W4 1QZ
Tel: 0181 747 3510
(kitchen sink, page 99)

Inventory
26-34 High Street Kensington
London W8 4PF
Tel: 0171 937 2626
(accessories, page 37)

Nordic Style
109 Lots Road
London SW10 0RN
Tel: 0171 351 1755
(chair, page 51; table, page 53)

The Pier
200 Tottenham Court Road
London W1P 0AD
Tel: 0171 436 9642
(chairs, pages 25 and 33;
bathroom accessories, page 77;
furniture, page 107)

The Shutter Shop
Queensbury House
Dilly Lane
Hertley
Wintney
Hampshire RG27 8E2
Tel: 01252 844575
(shutters, page 103)

Vitra
121 Milton Park
Abingdon
Oxon OX14 4SA
Tel: 01235 820400
(basin, page 73)

FABRICS
Anna French
343 King's Road
London SW3 5ES
Tel: 0171 351 1126
(page 41)

PAINTS AND GLAZES
Relics of Witney
35 Bridge Street
Witney
Nr Oxford
Tel: 01993 704 611
(traditional paints)

Casa Paints
PO Box 77
Thame
Oxon OX9 3FZ
Tel: 01296 770139
(Mediterranean colours)

Dulux
Wexham Road
Slough
Berks. SL2 5DS
Tel: 01753 550 555
(glazes and paints)

Paint Magic
48 Goldbourne Road
London W10 5PR
Tel: 0181 960 9960
(paints, glazes and materials)

Paint Works
5 Elgin Crescent
London W11 2JA
Tel: 0171 792 8012
(unusual range of colours and
paints)

Polyvine
Vine House
Rockhampton
Berkley
Gloucestershire
Tel: 01454 261 276
(acrylic scumble glaze, colouriz-
ers and varnishes)

Ray Munn
861-863 Fulham Road
London SW6 5HP
Tel: 0171 736 9876
(special colours in pre-tinted
glazes, paints and equipment)

Winsor & Newton
Whitefriars Avenue
Harrow
Middlesex HA3 5RH
Tel: 0181 427 4343
(oil and acrylic artist's colours)

MASKING TAPES
3M United Kingdom Plc.
3M House
PO Box 1
Bracknell
Berkshire RG12 1JU
Tel: 01344 858000
(low tack tapes)

Tesa Tape, Beiersdorf UK Ltd.
Tesa Division
Yeoman's Drive
Blakelands
Milton Keynes
Bucks. MK14 5LS
Tel: 01908 211 333
(Fleximask)

SPECIALIST SUPPLIERS
Jali Ltd.
Apsley House
Chartham
Nr. Canterbury
Kent CT4 7BR
Tel: 01227 831 710
(mouldings and radiator covers)

Liberon Waxes
Mountfield Industrial Estate
Learoyd Road
New Romney
Kent TN28 8XU
Tel: 01797 367555
(waxes and special finishes)

Wendy Cushing Trimmings
G7 Chelsea Harbour Design Centre
London SW10 OXE
Tel: 0171 351 5796

Winther Brown
Nobel Road
Ely Estate
London N18 BDX
Tel: 0181 803 3434
(dado rails, pages 28 and 44)

All stencils used and printed in this book are available by mail order ready cut from:
Yes-U-Can Stencils
57 Baron's Keep, Gliddon Road
London W14
Tel: 0171 603 3424
(for home use only, copyright Yes-U-Can)

Other similar stencils are available from:
The Stencil Library
Stocksfield Hall, Stocksfield
Northumberland NE43 7TN
Tel: 01661 844844

The Stencil Store
20-21 Heronsgate
Chorley Wood
Rickmansworth
Herts. WD36 2EB
Tel: 01923 285577

Elaine Green
Ladbroke Cottage
Penn Lane
Tamworth-in-Arden
West Midlands B94 5HJ
Tel: 01564 742 269

Acknowledgements

So many people helped me with this book, but my real lifeline was prayer. So my inexpressible first and biggest thank you has to be to my Heavenly Father who answered all my requests in Jesus' name and made the work such fun and so worry free, putting talented people in my way who generously shared their insights and expertise.

Eric Sharp, who is a serious mural painter, was one of them. He offered many useful tips and inspired me with his contagious enthusiasm. Yes-U-Can Stencils helped develop new designs with me at amazing speed for the mural projects. Mick Flynn at The Stencil Store was always willing to back me up with new products. Saleena Khara, also from The Stencil Store, gave me invaluable hands-on help. Eleanor Wright from The Chelsea School of Art and Justin Aggatt worked tirelessly painting photographic sets.

I am indebted to Fiona Eaton and Ali Myer, the patient and talented team at David & Charles who were endlessly helpful and encouraging. I am immensely grateful to Lizzie Orme who filled the photographs with sunshine and Sussie Bell who worked fastidiously to make the step-by-step photography so clear. I am so grateful to my husband Andrew, and two boys, Harry and Robert, for their unqualified positive encouragement, which I needed. They never once complained about their house being used as a photographic studio.

Finally, I am indebted to the companies who generously supplied materials and loaned products to make the book possible. Their names appear in the suppliers list.

Index